The Irish Uprising

With a foreword by Eamon de Valera

1916-1922

A CBS Legacy Collection Book/Produced by Goddard Lieberson

Distributed by The Macmillan Company

Contents

Foreword

This Easter we are bringing to our minds the Easter of fifty years ago, and are seeking to honor the men who at that time gave or risked their lives that Ireland might be free.

We wish to honor, in particular, the seven brave men who, despite all the deterrents, made the decision to assert, once more in arms, our nation's right to sovereign independence. It was a fateful decision which we now know to have been one of the boldest and most far-reaching in our history.

These were all good men, fully alive to their responsibilities, and it was only the firmest conviction, the fullest faith and love of country that prompted their action. Their single-mindedness and unselfishness, their sacrifice and the sacrifices of the others who gave their lives in the Uprising inspired the national resurgence which followed. May the good God have them all in His keeping.

Time has proved these men to have been prophets. They foresaw what few could then have foreseen, and to their foresight and their insight into the hearts of our people, under God's favor, we owe the privileges we enjoy here today.

Political freedom alone was not the ultimate goal. It was to be, rather, the enabling condition for the gradual building up of a community in which an ever increasing number of its members, relieved from the pressure of exacting economic demands, would be free to devote themselves more and more to the mind and spirit, and so, able to have the happiness of a full life. Our nation could then become again, as it was for centuries in the past, a great intellectual and missionary center from which would go forth the satisfying saving truths of Divine Revelation, as well as the fruits of the ripest secular knowledge.

We cannot adequately honor the men of 1916 if we do not work and strive to bring about the Ireland of their desire. For this each one of us must do his part, and though the tasks immediately before us now are different from those of fifty years ago, we can have today, if we are sufficiently devoted and our will be firm, a national resurgence comparable to that which followed 1916: we can have our people united as a family—a nation of brothers—each working in industrial harmony, not for himself only, but for the good of all. We could then march forward confidently to that exaltation of our nation amongst the nations to which the men of 1916 pledged themselves.

In the realization of all this our national language has a vital role. Language is a chief characteristic of nationhood—the embodiment, as it were, of the nation's personality and the closest bond between its people. No nation with a language of its own would willingly abandon it. The peoples of Denmark, Holland, Norway, for example, learn and know well one or more other languages, as we should, of course, for the sake of world communication, commerce, and for cultural purposes; but they would never abandon their native language, the language of their ancestors, the language which enshrines all the memories of their past. They know that without it they would sink into an amorphous cosmopolitanism—without a past, or a distinguishable future. To avoid such a fate, we of this generation must see to it that our language lives. That would be the resolve of the men and women of 1916. Will it not be the resolve of the young men and women of 1966?

Eamon de Valera

Eamon de Valera
President of Ireland
Easter, 1966

Prelude–
Mixed with Memories of Dublin

WHAT are we to make of the Irish? The picture has become so beclouded by passions, injustices, and violence, that we are no longer certain just how we may describe these complicated people. Adding to the confusion are the overwhelmingly white and black — no pastels for Ireland — cliché caricatures which range from the good old "Paddy" with clay pipe, top hat, shillelagh, and idiotic grin (in short, the vaudeville Irishman whose image was too long preserved in the United States) to turtleneck-sweatered intellectuals of either uncertain or red-hot politics, tough party bosses and their thugs, priests, ascetics, and, certainly not least of all, garrulous whiskey imbibers. A very exciting stew, indeed.

But where is Ireland in all of this? A large part of it disappears: certainly that vast panorama stretching back to an antiquity which archeologists now place at 2,000 B.C. The excitements of modern Irish history tend to make us forget that the monastic communities of the early Irish Church were important centers of learning and arts which represented the beginning of a great scholarly tradition. Indeed, for five-and-a-half centuries after the foundation of the Monastic University of Clonmacnois in A.D. 548, Ireland was by far the cultural leader, not only for her immediate neighbors, the English, but for continental Europe as well; and for a period, it was customary for great families to send their scholar-sons to Ireland for an education.

But, alas, as it turned out there were many others besides scholars who went to Ireland. She seemed to have developed a fatal attraction for visitors (mostly armed) whether they were Norsemen, Normans, or English. And it started early—in the first half of the 9th century—as if intended to provide the Irish with a long experience for their later dealings with the English. Rebellion as a normal reaction was early planted in the Irish character, and succeeding generations of invaders always found the Irish to be exactly what history had trained them to be—a thorn in the side. Henry VIII, a specialist in thorns, saved for Ireland, in his attempt to Anglicize her, his heaviest and bloodiest hand. But, as was to be the case again and again, the heavier and bloodier the hand, the less effective it was: and in this case particularly, since this invasion was identified with a new and alien Protestant religion, which challenged the integrity of an ancient Catholic faith. Queen Elizabeth's deputies continued the cruel game, massacring whole families in Ireland who were considered politically dangerous, and after her, James I considered outright colonization to be the only and best means for subjugating the Irish.

Soon after, the religious lines became clearly drawn as terrible wars developed between the new settlers and the Roman Catholic Anglo-Irish. When, in 1649, Oliver Cromwell arrived to reconquer in his own behalf the recalcitrant Irish, he too used a frightful military intimidation as his chief means for doing so. In the 1652 Act of Settlement, over ten million acres of estates owned by Catholics were confiscated and transferred to English owners. These were never returned, even after the Restoration, when a somewhat easier tone was taken, and the Catholics of Ireland became a dispossessed, persecuted people.

If the words "persecution" or "subjugation" seem strong, consider the terrible penal laws which were promulgated around the beginning of the 18th century. Under this penal code (which victimized about three-fourths of the nation) the

by Goddard Lieberson

Catholics in Ireland had no suffrage; they were barred from corporations, the magistracy, the bar, the bench, grand juries, vestries; and they could not be sheriffs, gamekeepers, or constables. They were forbidden to possess arms, or to own a horse of the value of more than £5, and any Protestant, upon payment of the £5, could appropriate the horse of his Catholic neighbor. Catholic education was absolutely and unlimitedly proscribed; no Catholic could buy land, or inherit it, or even receive it as a gift from a Protestant. All Catholic archbishops, bishops, deans and vicars-general were ordered to leave the country by a specified date. If after that date they were discovered, they were to be first imprisond and then banished, and if they were ever to return, they were guilty of high treason and liable to be hanged, disembowelled and quartered. There was a reward of £50 to anyone securing the conviction of any Catholic archbishop, bishop, dean, or vicar-general. Such provisions—relegating Catholics to a persecuted, secondary citizenship—finally, of course, divided the Irish on religious lines (although in the century that followed Scotch and Irish Presbyterians were also to experience intolerance at the hands of the Established Church of Ireland, or England).

Little wonder, then, that for many Irish, emigration seemed the only hope and that, in America by 1790, nearly ten per cent of the white population were of Irish origin. The Irish quickly identified themselves with the American Revolution, and one contemporary English estimate had it that half the American army was from Ireland. Undoubtedly, this was the beginning of the later close association of America with Irish republicanism.

Throughout Ireland's history the relentlessly unchanging element in the country's chemical mixture has been its characteristic reaction to persecution. One need hardly mention the dreadful potato famine of the mid-19th century—which, in its combination of death by starvation and disease and the further mass emigration to the United States that followed, reduced the population of Ireland by nearly two million people in the space of six years. Nor—as was brutally clear at least to the Irish themselves—was the famine an act of God, but rather of an administration that left people to live or die by the potato in a land where grain and beef were growing in abundance. But that policy was ultimately to reap its own reward. For the attempted separation of Irish society into landlords and serfs inevitably resulted in that imbalance which made most of those who remained in Ireland Irishmen before anything else. Thus the first stirrings of Irish republicanism and Irish nationalism (whether artistic or political) were deeply participated in by Protestants and Anglo-Irish, and, indeed, a good deal of the national leadership sprang from these groups. This is only one of the many strange, contradictory aspects of Irish history. But as the idea of republicanism began to crystallize, it was bound to collect to itself men from all different backgrounds; the central issue of Irish independence was too important to tolerate any division based on other prejudices.

In the midst of the serious atmosphere of revolt —and nothing, after all, can finally be more serious than risks of life and limb—the Irish were not without their usual cachinnators. When Sean T. O'Kelly (who was later to be President of Ireland and who is best described by the Irish term, "a darling man") went to America to raise money for the rebellion, his contact turned out to be a man who, though an ardent supporter of Irish republicanism, was close to being stone deaf. It must have been difficult to shout in conspiratorial tones! And when, as he recounts later in this book, Sean T. finally did get the money, it was delivered to him by yet another eccentric Irishman who brought English gold sovereigns because he was tickled by the irony of financing a rebellion in the coin of the realm. What was lost on this fellow was the idea that even if poor Sean T. could successfully transport these heavy boxes across the ocean, he must then depend upon the unlikely possibility of meeting a customs agent who might look upon a trunk full of gold coins as quite normal luggage.

When I was recently in Dublin, I had a view of yet a different kind of humor in connection with the uprising; what the Germans call *"Galgenhumor"*—gallows humor. I heard of it during one of my visits to the same Sean T. O'Kelly while he was in the hospital in Dublin. He was talking of the days just after the surrender when all of the leaders of the Easter Rising, or, as it must have seemed, anyone having anything to do with Irish republicanism, was in jail. The group that Sean T. was in included, among others prominent in the uprising, Eamon de Valera. There were twenty prisoners in one big barrack room, and all fully expected to be shot. Somebody suggested that they pass the time by having a mock court martial of de Valera that night. The oldest among them, Count Plunkett, father of Joseph Mary, was appointed to be the judge. A bucket was turned upside down, a blanket placed over it, and this was to be used as the judge's seat. Sean T. turned to one of the prisoners, Larry O'Neil, the Lord Mayor of Dublin, and said, "Larry, you be the prosecutor." "I will not," said he. "I wouldn't prosecute. I'll defend him." In fact, nobody would take on the prosecution, and as Sean T. said ruefully, "I had to do it myself. I prosecuted de Valera." When it came to the finish of the trial, after a long peroration defending de Valera, the judge refused to go any further; he could not bring himself to condemn "Dev" to death. But the judge was alone in his squeamishness; the rest of them started cutting the buttons off de Valera's clothes as souvenirs. A strange way to spend the night before an expected execution! But also strange is what next happened in Sean T.'s hospital room; just as he ended this story, there was a knock on the door, it opened, and there stood President de Valera, who had come to visit. His large frame filled the door. I had been with him the day before, but seeing him again re-emphasized how physically imposing a man he is, in spite of his years. His only apparent weakness is a poorish eyesight, and upon seeing my outline, but not my face, he thought at first that he was in the wrong room, but Sean T.'s voice reassured him. Then he assumed that I was the visiting doctor! However, we finally got it all sorted out, and he came in.

Seeing these two old gentlemen together (they are both in their 84th year, as of this writing, separated by some few months only) was indeed touching. De Valera went over to Sean T. and said, "I hear you're going home today. How do you feel?" And Sean T. told him, as he had told me, that he had had a very bad night, and that the medicine didn't work as far as relieving the pain of his sciatica, and that finally at four A.M. (and this he said slyly) he had been forced to take some whiskey. De Valera said, "Didn't you try some brandy? My doctor has told me to take it," and Sean T. answered quickly, "I took both."

But so much of this bears the sweetness and nostalgia of afterthought spanning fifty years. What of the Rising itself—certainly not only material for the rich memories of those who survived and lived to see victory of a kind. Many were to be killed in the month after Easter Monday. And though ultimately it can be said to have been a political success, in its own time the uprising was an enterprise doomed at the outset. Poorly organized, orders given and then countermanded, too few men, too few guns and of the wrong kind, the leaders themselves inexperienced—poetical men, for the most part, many of whom found the use of violence a repellent idea but who were yet forced suddenly into assuming a military stance they barely knew how to take.

One has only to look at the seven men who signed the Proclamation of the Republic on that fateful Monday afternoon to understand how warfare could have been but a last resort. Of the seven, I don't believe any one of them had ever shot much more than a rabbit, and perhaps even that under protest. To think of them as military men must have taken a rather large stretch of the imagination. Yet here was Padraic Pearse, a poet and dramatist, in the role of the Commander General of the Irish Republican forces and President of the Provisional Government. With him in signing the Proclamation were: Thomas MacDonagh, thirty-eight, also a poet, member of the Gaelic League, who wrote a play for the Abbey Theater, and, of all things, a study of Thomas Campion; Eamonn Ceannt, thirty-four, a clerk in the city treasury department, beyond everything else Irish in his feelings, a performer on the Irish warpipes and so expert that he went to the Vatican to play them for Pope Saint Pius X; Joseph Mary Plunkett, twenty-nine, descendant of an illustrious family, son of a Papal Count, a gentle, delicate man, deeply Catholic, who daily read Saint Theresa of Avila, Saint John of the Cross, and Saint Thomas Aquinas; Sean MacDermott, thirty-two, perhaps most widely known of the Irish Volunteers, who had hoped to be a teacher but who had worked as a bar man and then as a tram driver in order to devote himself completely to his work for Irish freedom; James Connolly, forty-six, a socialist and union organizer whose unending hope was for better conditions for the working men and women of Ireland, and, ex-cept for his devotion to the "cause" quite unlike most of his comrades in arms (but he knew the meanings of things and it was he who said, "From the moment that the first shot is fired, there will be no longer Volunteers or Citizen Army, but only the Army of the Irish Republic"); and finally there was Thomas Clarke, fifty-eight, the oldest of the group—a gentle-appearing man, marked by fifteen-and-a-half years of intense suffering in English jails but undaunted, and perhaps the chief moving force behind the Rising, a good part of which was organized at meetings in his little tobacco shop in Parnell Street. And all of them would be shot in Kilmainham Jail in the early days of May. After a long series of mistakes, these executions were to be the greatest of England's blunders in her handling of the Irish problem.

In Dublin, on Easter Monday morning, parties of men in arms marched from Liberty Hall on their way to take possession of the General Post Office in O'Connell Street. Pearse and James Connolly were in the lead, but the main body of the Volunteer army did not follow their leaders to the General Post Office. They marched in three sections: one, under Captain Sean Connolly, went straight to Dublin Castle where Connolly was shot dead not long afterwards. The other sections under Michael Mallin, with the famous Countess Markievicz as his second in command, marched to St. Stephen's Green where they divided. Here, groups of Volunteers came into contact with the Irish public, who were by no means friendly. The Volunteers themselves must have thought it a rum way to start an uprising—having to clear the people out of St. Stephen's Green where they were enjoying themselves. Many of the ladies pushing perambulators and with children running about their skirts were indignant and threatened to call the police. What a curious sight this all must have been: on the one side, the puzzled public, and on the other, this amateur "army" accompanied by a number of women patriots acting as nurses, runners, and searching here and there for food supplies. Those Dubliners not involved were walking around staring at what certainly must have seemed to them a perfectly mad group of people, inside the Post Office as well as in the Green. And mixed into all of this were mothers trying to locate their sons and friends of the Volunteers bringing food packages. In general, the public was at first quiet, out of indifference or, very likely in some cases, friendliness. At the taking of the Post Office, the indifference was to be tinged with hostility and undoubtedly turned to outright consternation when the fighting began.

Many of the Volunteers were clambering over the roofs at the corners of the Green. One of them reported that on the roof he opened a trap-door to see if there was a way out, and an angry voice yelled up, "What the devil are you doing up there?" When he indicated his gun and explained that some men would probably be going out through the house shortly and that they would try to make as little disturbance as they could, would take nothing, and would get out on the street as quickly as possible, the man said, "All right, but don't wake the children." Sometimes on the street corners there would be little gatherings of young girls—this was particularly so at the corner where the Russell Hotel stands—and there they would stand, hurling abusive language at the Volunteers. There seemed not to have been much wanton destruction. One of the Volunteers did, however, remember that he saw a young boy (who should not have been there at all) ripping a portrait of Queen Victoria to pieces. Mallin, the Commandant, was furious when he saw this, and announced that he would shoot any man

who damaged any work of art.

It was certainly not a well-organized army. One man reported that he was told to stay wide awake and on guard with four other men in the room, and to his amazement the four other men promptly curled up on the floor and, though they had promised to keep awake, were snoring in a few minutes. They soon awoke, however, when snipers' bullets came through the window.

No one was really prepared for what had been undertaken. Most of the fighters went for days without sleeping or washing, and many went without eating. All over the city little groups were isolated, not really knowing what was going on. Bright skies lit by the fires led some of them to believe that Dublin was finished forever, and in their filthy condition, the hunger and thirst were now augmented by depression. In the middle of all of this, the elegant and really quite beautiful Countess Markievicz calmly asked somebody for a "bayonet or something"—"some stabbing instrument"—in case there were action at close quarters!

It must from the outset have been apparent to all except the most self-mesmerized of the republicans that this uprising could not succeed as a military venture. It did, however, make its tragic statement. And after seven days of fighting during which hopelessly outnumbered groups were reduced to holding sniper positions—and to such extremities as trying to catch hand grenades being hurled at them in order to throw them back—surrender was inevitable. And, as the hungry fight-worn Irish lads gave up, neither side could really know what was in store for them. Who were these young lads? Most of them were between the ages of eighteen and twenty-five. They began the fight with a light-heartedness that very quickly turned grim. They had come from all walks of life in Ireland, and as one of them later said, ". . . there was in Dublin a kind of natural graduation, which lead to participation in the Rising for lads of the more advanced national views. One usually began by playing Gaelic football or hurling; from that, the next step was to the Gaelic League; from that again to the Sinn Fein movement, and later to the Irish Volunteer movement. For relaxation we attended the Abbey Theater. We bought nothing but the Irish-made goods and scorned those who bought goods made in England. With that background it was rather a natural progression to participation in the Rising . . . which was a gallant but hopeless venture which could only end in early defeat."

Pearse in his idealism had hoped that he would be able to surrender for everybody and take the full burden of their guilt upon himself. This as we know was not to be. Some who surrendered did so unnecessarily, out of a kind of naivety: to escape they had but to mingle with the crowd, since most of them were in civilian clothes. Presumably, they thought themselves in honor bound by the surrender of their commanders to make a proper surrender, so they stolidly went forward to meet their captors. During these surrender marches, as they were being led off to jail, they found a good deal of the public was not with them, and there were shouted instructions to the British soldiers to "stick your bayonets in the bloody barstards." At this point in Irish history, a large "establishment" wanted nothing to do with any Rising. Although there were individual priests sympathetic to republicanism, the main body of the Church was not in favor of the uprising. Taking the view of the time, it was probably a conservative and righteous point of view to stick with the Parliamentary party and its hopes for rational dealing with England.

I know that these days it is the fashion among some of the younger Dubliners to be a bit blasé and bored about "the Rising." And it does seem at times that there are enough people in Dublin now claiming to have been with Pearse and Connolly in the Post Office to have filled not only the Dublin Post Office but all of the post offices in Ireland, and a few in England as well. For someone living in Ireland, then, perhaps there is apt to be a little too much talk and a little too much song about the Rising for it to remain a serious subject. But how could such an event not have left a persisting memory with those who had been in the thick of it?

The day following the incident in the hospital, I was to leave Dublin, and early that morning I had a telephone call from President de Valera. He wanted to send me a book that he thought I should read. He also asked if I had been told what charge was levied against him in the mock court martial. "I was," he said, "being tried as the Pretender to the Throne of the Muglands"—a series of uninhabitable rocks near Dalkey Islands, in Dublin Bay, and as unlikely a place to have either a throne or a pretender as one could imagine.

There is no doubting the charismatic appeal of de Valera. When he received me at Aras an Uachtarian in Phoenix Park, he stood straight and as solid as a rock, and when he spoke, he did so with a precision and certitude that made it easy to remember he had begun his career as a teacher and a mathematician. Nor was I surprised when he told me that he keeps current with mathematics and mathematical physics, has new works in the field read to him, and often works out problems on a blackboard for his mental exercise.

I had wanted particularly to hear about his dealings with Lloyd George and asked him if he had encountered the now-legendary force of Lloyd George's personal wiles. Yes, indeed, he had encountered it; at their first meeting, for instance, Lloyd George had opened the discussion with a reference to "We Celts. . . ." De Valera, one can imagine—and probably not the least by Irish politics itself—had been well schooled in remaining impervious to this particular form of political art. But however obdurate in this regard, de Valera was not in those days without a certain innocence. He believed, he said, that in negotiating with the British Prime Minister he was dealing with a man entirely free to make his own decisions. Having subsequently come to exercise power himself, he came also to realize something of what must have been the complicated system of checks and limits on Lloyd George's freedom to act. But if, as de Valera admits, he was rather more naive then than he could be today, this admission is not meant in any way to excuse Lloyd George, who later in their meeting threatened, "I can put a soldier in Ireland for every man, woman, and child there." And de Valera's answer to his remark was, "Yes, but you must keep them there." Thus the particular course of British policy with respect to Lloyd George's fellow-"Celts" in Ireland seems to have been one in which he at the very least fully concurred.

So here we are fifty years later, still rehearsing the old arguments, arguments rendered only the more tangled and poignant by the bloody Civil War that was to take place only a few years after the Rising. Brendan Behan was once quoted as saying (although it might be a folk saying), "If it were raining soup the Irish would come out of their houses with forks in their hands"—which perhaps would in those days of 1916 have seemed to many people to sum up the events in Dublin. But we know now that the Easter Rising served ultimately to define a national purpose and create a national will that could not have been defined or created in any other way. □

TARA IS GRASS

The world hath conquered, the wind hath scattered like dust
Alexander, Caesar, and all that shared their sway:
Tara is grass, and behold how Troy lieth low—
And even the English, perchance their hour will come.

From the 18th-century Gaelic/Translated by Padraic Pearse

Citizens of Galway at their peaceful pursuits—around the turn of the 20th century.

The Springs of 1916

THE Easter Rising of 1916 burst with unexpected suddenness on a politically complacent Ireland. Yet it was no mushroom growth springing up overnight. It had its origins in a revival of national feeling which had molded a new generation. Its causes lay in a reaction to the futile politics of internecine strife between rival parties after the death of Charles Stewart Parnell in 1891. In a sense it was a turning away from politics and a casting back to the past—to the language, music and literature of previous generations.

The 19th century had witnessed the decay of the national language and of national pastimes. Ireland was fast being absorbed into the British Empire, and its own identity being lost. There were some people who reacted against this trend but it was not until the end of the century that an effort was made to reverse the process. Probably the most influential body to face the task was the Gaelic League founded by Dr. Douglas Hyde in 1893. A year before, in a lecture to the National Literary Society, he declared his views: *"In Anglicising ourselves wholesale we have thrown away with a light heart the best claim which we have upon the world's recognition of us as a separate nationality.... In order to de-Anglicise ourselves we must at once arrest the decay of the language. ... We must strive to cultivate everything that is most racial, most smacking of the soil, most Gaelic, most Irish because, in spite of the little admixture of Saxon blood in the northeast corner, this island is, and will ever remain, Celtic at the core.... I believe it is our Gaelic past which, though the Irish race does not recognise it just at present, is really at the bottom of the Irish heart, and prevents us becoming citizens of the Empire."*

The Gaelic League was the instrument to create the new spirit.

Padraic Pearse was later to write: *"If there is one thing that has become plainer than another it is that when the seven met in O'Connell Street to found the Gaelic League they were commencing ... not a revolt but a revolution."*

There is a mystic significance associated with the number seven, and the seven men of 1893 were to be followed by yet another seven, of whom Pearse was to be one—the seven signatories of the Proclamation of the Irish Republic in 1916. But in 1893 that day seemed a long way off and the seven founders of 1893 did not dream that from their actions would stem a movement which was to create a new Ireland. Nevertheless it was true.

As year succeeded year the Gaelic League grew and spread throughout Ireland. Branches were formed in which not only the Irish language but Irish history as well were taught. Traditions of the past were revived and the Gaelic League classes were not only places of study but of entertainment. Irish music was played and Irish songs sung. Traditional dances were practiced. The doctrine of Irishness was inculcated. All of this was non-political in intent but in practice it could not be divorced from politics. It molded a new generation whose outlook was fundamentally Irish. It was only a matter of time before that attitude would reflect itself in the political field. The Irish Parliamentarians, however, carried on their politics largely unaware of the great changes that were taking place among the people of Ireland. While they still aimed at winning Home Rule, there was a growing body of opinion which in the logic of its outlook would not be satisfied with anything less than complete independence.

Of course it was not clear at the time that the logical conclusion of the Gaelic League outlook was something more than a limited Home Rule. There were some like the poet, William Rooney, who railed at the Gaelic League's rule against in-

by Thomas P. O'Neill

Grafton Street, Dublin, 1913.

terfering in politics. For the most part, however, Douglas Hyde and his associates merely pursued their course, unwittingly creating a revolution.

The movement for the revival of the Irish language was to be a powerhouse radiating its influence in many directions. Culturally one of its most significant effects was the change which it brought about in Anglo-Irish literature. The Irish literary revival largely centered around the Abbey Theater and its leaders were George Moore, William Butler Yeats, Lady Gregory and John Millington Synge. They all came under the influence of the language movement. George Moore himself in a speech to the Irish Literary Theater in 1900 stated his opinions: *"I do not say that without our language we shall become English. I do not say it, though I fear that the distinction of language is, perhaps, the most essential of all distinctions, for it is by means of language that the characteristics of race are preserved. . . . My fellow countrymen, the language hovers on the verge of the grave, and what you have to remember is that when the language is dead the soul of Cuchulain, which we all still share a little, will have vanished."*

Reaching back into Irish mythology for its heroes, such as Cuchulain, the literary movement provided a new inspiration for an old dream.

National sentiment in Ireland had long found a romantic refuge, and the literary movement was even more romantic than the language revival. Writers like Yeats revolted against the tradition of earlier national poets whose aim was political. In his writings he would preach no political gospel. His writing was purely literary. *"I will not,"* he wrote, *"have all my readers with me when I say that no writer, no artist, even though he choose Brian Boroimhe or St. Patrick for his subject, should try to make his work popular. Once he has chosen his subject he must think of nothing but giving it such expression as will please himself. . . ."* There was to be, for William Butler Yeats, no subordination of arts and letters to political ends.

Nonetheless the literary revival was political. It inspired the imagination. It recreated the ancient heroes and it won new admirers for the beautiful woman who in tradition personified Ireland—Cathleen Ni Houlihan. Yeats might not see it any more than did Hyde but together they were making the mind of a new generation. Moore might resist the fatal beauty for whom men were a willing sacrifice. *"I begin to tremble,"* he wrote in "Hail and Farewell," *"lest the terrible Cathleen Ni Houlihan might overtake me. She had come out of that arid plain, out of the mist, to tempt me, to soothe me with forgetfulness that*

HOME RULE NEAR

ASQUITH INTRODUCES GOVERNMENT OF IRELAND BILL

TENSION IN THE HOUSE OF COMMONS

The terms of Mr. Asquith's bill to provide Home Rule for Ireland have finally been disclosed. Though far from a program for complete self-government, it is felt by the Prime Minister that this new measure will satisfy the Nationalists while at the same time obvi-

Home Rule for Ireland had been a pending issue in British
Commons since 1886, when Gladstone introduced it.
By 1912, with Asquith and the Liberals in power,
a limited measure of Irish self-determination seemed a surety.

"Trust the Old Party, and Home Rule next year"—John Redmond, leader of the Irish Parliamentary Party, addresses a meeting at the Parnell Monument, Dublin, 1912. Also at this meeting was national patriot Padraic Pearse, who said, "We have no wish to destroy the British, we only want our freedom."

it is the plain duty of every Irishman to dissociate himself from all memories of Ireland."

Yeats might write his poetry on a detached artistic level avoiding to some extent the realities of the romanticism which he did not recognize. He could write: *"We have all bent low and low and kissed/the quiet feet/Of Cathleen, the daughter of Houlihan"* without realizing or admitting the consequences of such homage.

Now, with the advantage of hindsight, one wonders that men were so blind—that Yeats in 1913 could blandly compose the lines: *"Was it for this the wild geese spread/The grey wing upon every tide;/For this that all that blood was shed,/For this that Edward Fitzgerald died,/And Robert Emmet and Wolfe Tone,/All that delirium of the brave?/Romantic Ireland's dead and gone,/It's with O'Leary in the grave."*

Romantic Ireland had never been more alive and Yeats had been one of those who had resuscitated it. His poetic question was one which was already rearing its head in other minds—was it for limited Home Rule that the patriots of the past had given their lives? The question was not voiced but the spirit of the age was such that it was certainly one which must arise.

One of the reasons why the whole basis of Home Rule would be questioned lay in the economic ramifications of the cultural movement which was sweeping the country. At the head of its notepaper the Gaelic League carried the motto—SINN FEIN. President de Valera was, in later years, to define its meaning: *"Sinn Fein means literally 'We Ourselves.' It was chosen as a motto of self-reliance—the motto of those who long ago said it was vain to hope for a change of heart in the governments of England but who turned towards, and had full confidence in, the strength and determination of the people of Ireland. Those who pose as experts now in rendering the motto as 'Ourselves Alone,' twisting it to mean a doctrine of selfish isolation, are precisely those who some time ago would deem it a mark of inferiority to profess any acquaintance with the Irish language."*

This self-reliant attitude was seen in the vitality of urban industrial development and in the rural co-operative movement. The latter was the brain-child of Sir Horace Plunkett, who, like most of his contemporaries, underestimated the forces loosed around him. Nevertheless, he realized that his co-operative societies did not live in isolation. *"Of this language movement,"* he wrote, *"I am myself but an outside observer, having been forced to devote nearly all my time and energies to a variety of attempts which aim at doing in the industrial sphere much of the same work*

(Above) Ulster Volunteers in training.

*Northern Protestants pledged absolute opposition to Home Rule,
demanded to retain union with England. In the six Unionist
counties, called Ulster, a volunteer army was organized, and
threatened insurrection at the institution of a Dublin Parliament.*

Edward Carson, K.C., who, as Parliamentary spokesman for the Northern Protestant Unionists' opposition to Home Rule,
was Redmond's counterpart in Ulster, denounces Home Rule before a meeting in Belfast.

as that which the Gaelic movement attempts in the intellectual sphere—the rehabilitation of Ireland from within."

Success attended the co-operative societies, of which more than eight hundred were scattered through the country within nine years of Plunkett's Irish Agricultural Organization Society in 1894. This was the body which was to be the guide and mentor of agricultural co-operation in Ireland. Plunkett was no more a politician than was Hyde or Yeats. He did not understand the politics of nationalism but he contributed to it with his doctrine of self-reliance.

More vigorous, and more political too, was the journalist, D. P. Moran. Like William Rooney he wanted a more vigorous and virile Gaelic League than that visualized by Hyde. He saw that the League was more than a language or literary movement. It could turn the mind of Ireland and pave the way for industrial development. Not the least important of his activities was his relentless "Buy Irish" campaign which afforded voluntary protection to Irish industry. He was the father of an industrial movement based on an expansion of Hyde's cultural Irish Irelandism.

Of course, the varied streams which made up the tide of national feeling that was building up in the early years of this century did not always run smoothly. There were frictions and discords. Moran could denounce Yeats as "one of the most glaring frauds that the credulous Irish people had ever swallowed." Yet all the streams ran together and mingled, their diversity lost in the flood-tide which they created. It was natural that they should, for in fact they were never separate streams. Each owed something to the other; they overlapped and intertwined. The secretary of the co-operative movement who cycled indefatigably all over Ireland in the service of Plunkett's prosaic creameries was AE (George Russell), poet and author, a link between the literary revival and the material regeneration. It was a time when poets and dreamers became practical men and practical men became dreamers.

The writers of Irish Ireland in those years sounded an apocalyptic note. They all preached that it was now or never for the Gael. They were convinced of the urgency of the moment, of the need for immediate action to save the language, to build a nation. Thus it was that, with the threat to Home Rule in 1913, a new movement began, a militant movement in tune with the militant past which had been resurrected by the Gaelic League and the literature of the Celtic Twilight: the Irish Volunteers.

There had always been a hard core of militants in Ireland who felt that freedom would never be

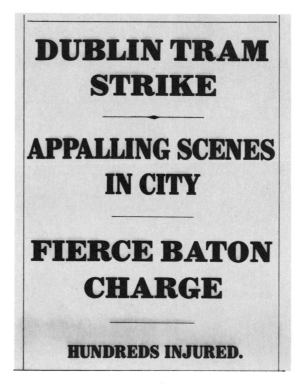

DUBLIN TRAM STRIKE

APPALLING SCENES IN CITY

FIERCE BATON CHARGE

HUNDREDS INJURED.

*In August 1913 police charged a meeting of the Irish Transport
and General Workers Union, then on strike against the tramways.
The strike was to be broken in 1914, but in the meantime
was to consolidate nationalist feeling among the workers and
lead to their organizing a Citizen Army.*

Dublin Metropolitan Police and Royal Irish Constabulary charging Transport Workers' Union meeting in O'Connell Street, after which Union's leader, Jim Larkin, was to be taken to prison.

REASONS WHY

YOU SHOULD JOIN

The Irish Citizen Army.

BECAUSE It pledges its members to work for, organise for, drill for and fight for **an Independent Ireland.**

BECAUSE It places its reliance upon the only class that never betrayed Ireland—the Irish Working Class.

BECAUSE Having a definite aim to work for there is no fear of it being paralysed in the moment of action by divisions in its Executive Body.

BECAUSE It teaches that "the sole right of ownership of Ireland is vested in the people of Ireland, and that that full right of ownership may, and ought to be, enforced by any and all means that God hath put within the power of man."

BECAUSE It works in harmony with the Labour and true National Movements and thus embraces all that makes for Social Welfare and National Dignity.

Companies Wanted in Every District.

RECRUITS WANTED EVERY HOUR.

Apply for further information, Secretary, Citizen Army, Liberty Hall, Dublin.

Handbill distributed in 1913 calling for recruitment in the Irish Citizen Army.

(Right) Dublin youngsters reflect the growing martial spirit

achieved except by physical force. The resurgent spirit of the early 20th century was one not of their making but they were willing to use it, to direct it. Through the Irish Republican Brotherhood, a secret society to which they belonged, they were able partially to direct affairs in accordance with their lights. They were able to channel new enthusiasms into directions most suitable to their purpose—a completely independent Irish Republic. And with the founding of the Irish Volunteers they had a new weapon to their hands.

Perhaps there was exaggeration in Padraic Pearse's statement, early in 1914, "...that the Volunteer movement has sprung out of the language movement. It is one of a large and thriving family of youngsters of whom, whether it own them or not (and it is chary enough about owning some of them), the Gaelic League is undoubtedly the parent. The League has become a highly respectable member of society; it sits in high places and has cultured leisure. But it will be recognised in history as the most revolutionary influence that has ever come into Ireland. The Irish Revolution really began when the seven proto-Gaelic Leaguers met in O'Connell Street. Their deed of 1893 made our deed of 1913 possible. The germ of all future Irish history was in that back room."

Pearse saw what Hyde and Plunkett did not see,

that it was not necessary to have a definite political program in order to influence political thought and action. Prophetically he wrote: "We never meant to be Gaelic Leaguers and nothing more than Gaelic Leaguers. We meant to do something for Ireland, each in his own way.... As to what your work as an Irish Nationalist is to be, I cannot conjecture; I know what mine is to be, and would have you know yours and buckle yourself to it. And it may be (nay, it is) that yours and mine will lead us to a common meeting-place, and that on a certain day we shall stand together, with many more beside us, ready for a greater adventure than any of us has yet had, a trial and a triumph to be endured and achieved in common."

No longer was the work through the Gaelic League alone but through "the groups and the individuals that have arisen, or are arising, out of the Gaelic League."

The meeting-place which Pearse foresaw was still two and a half years away but the first step had been taken in the founding of the Irish Volunteer force at the Rotunda Rink in Dublin in November 1913. Young men filled with the glory of young Cuchulain joined an open military organization. Even this body could in a sense claim to be non-political, founded not to oust but strengthen the Home Rulers. "Ireland unarmed will attain just (Continued on page 18)

*Eoin MacNeill (below), Professor at University College, Dublin,
calls for the organization of a body of volunteers to defend
Irish freedom. At its inaugural meeting on November 25, 1913,
4000 men are to enroll—among them a young teacher of
mathematics named Eamon de Valera.*

Emmet Died to Free Ireland.

What are YOU doing towards this glorious object?

What can I do?

Join a Volunteer Company, which will train you to bear arms in Ireland's cause.

Do you live in the Rathmines District?

Are you Free on Friday Nights?

If so, D Company, 4th Batt. Dublin I. V., will welcome you at Larkfield, Kimmage (beside Mount Argus).

PROGRAMME OF TRAINING
(Each Friday Night):

8—9. Musketry (for each man) and Close or Extended Order Drill or Short Double.

9—9.30. Signalling or Bayonet Exercise.

9.30—9.45. General Physical Training, including Jumping, Vaulting, etc.

9.45—10. Short First Aid Lecture.

10. Announcements and Dismiss.

KEEP THIS TO BAIT YOUR FRIENDS WITH

Irish Volunteers seek with this appeal to enlarge their ranks.

1500 second-hand Mauser rifles and 49,000 rounds of ammunition are delivered secretly to the Irish Volunteers from a yacht in Howth Harbor, July 26, 1914. The guns are distributed then and there to each man. On the march back to Dublin the police will attempt, but unsuccessfully, to seize the arms.

"We must accustom ourselves to the thought of arms, to the sight of arms, to the use of arms."—Padraic Pearse.

*"England's Difficulty is Ireland's Opportunity" had since the
mid-19th century been a motto of Irish nationalists.
Now, with England about to be embroiled in a great and
costly war, there were stirrings of hope in Dublin that Ireland
might in one way or another benefit from her present difficulties.*

as much freedom as it is convenient for England to give her," wrote Pearse. *"Ireland armed will attain ultimately just as much freedom as she wants."*

This was the spirit in which the Irish Volunteers were formed. The heroic spirit evoked by the resurgence of the preceding years, however, was already coming to fruition. The threat of war lay over Europe and combined with a sacrificial outlook in youths of that generation to harden their purpose. The Parliamentarians had eschewed physical force in Ireland's cause. Now there were men to preach: *"Bloodshed is a cleansing and sanctifying thing, and the nation which regards it as the final horror has lost its manhood. There are many things more horrible than bloodshed; and slavery is one of them."*

Not all saw the challenge in the same way, but there were men prepared to embark on a course which must inevitably end in battle. Pearse's original Irish poem translated by Thomas MacDonagh seems to have had a prophetic quality: *"I set my face/To the road here before me,/To the work I see,/To the death that I shall get."*

Both Pearse and MacDonagh were to be signatories of the Proclamation of The Irish Republic at Easter 1916, and both were to face the firing squads unflinchingly in Kilmainham Jail afterwards.

ENGLAND DECLARES WAR ON GERMANY.

BRITISH ULTIMATUM ON BELGIAN NEUTRALITY.

MR. ASQUITH'S GRAVE STATEMENT.

IRELAND RESPONDS TO MOBILIZATION

The declaration, yesterday, by Sir Edward Grey in the House of Commons of the Government's decision to declare war on Germany was greeted by the MP's in a mood of sobriety, determination, and deep pride. Mr. John Redmond rose and assured the Government that they might with all confidence withdraw their

Step by step the revolutionary pace quickened. There may have been poetic license in some of the writings but the spirit had been roused and actions were speaking louder than words. If the formation of the Volunteers was a decisive step, so too was the arming of them by the landing of arms at Howth and Kilcoole in the summer of 1914. More decisive still was the refusal of a portion of the Volunteers to follow Redmond when war broke out in Europe. The men who stood firm on that occasion were a minority but they were a dedicated body. As Pearse called on them at the graveside of the dead hero of the last insurrection in Ireland, Jeremiah O'Donovan Rossa, to renew their baptismal vows he explained that he was *"... speaking on behalf of a new generation that has been re-baptised in the Fenian faith, and that has accepted the responsibility of carrying out the Fenian programme."*

For men such as Pearse nationalism had a religious tone, not in a sectarian sense, but in the fervor which it aroused. He drew many parallels between love of country and love of God. The choice of Easter as the time for the Rising emphasized the spiritual aspect of the patriotism of the leaders. When seven men signed the 1916 proclamation they may not have been such visionaries as their poetry and writings *(Continued on page 24)*

(Right) British recruiting poster appeals for Irish assistance in the war against Germany.

AN ENQUIRY FROM THE FRONT

"When are the other boys COMING?"

Redmond in Commons had pledged Ireland's support in the war,
and following him, some 200,000 volunteers were to join the
British army in the course of the war. Only 11,000 or
12,000 men remained with MacNeill in the Irish Volunteers.

A British recruiting officer makes his appeal to a crowd of Dubliners, and finds a volunteer.

James Connolly's Irish Citizen Army, shown here in front of Liberty Hall, makes known its neutrality on the question of British or German victory.

*Jeremiah O'Donovan Rossa, a hero of a by-now legendary rising
of the Fenians in 1867, who had suffered and languished in
English prisons, died in America in July of 1915.
His body was brought to Dublin for burial, and on August 1
thousands accompanied his hearse to Glasnevin Cemetery.*

might suggest. Pearse had written of the war in Europe that it had brought heroism back to the earth, that war was a terrible thing but not more terrible than the evils it would end. There was a tragic, sacrificial, note about his words: *"The old heart of the earth needed to be warmed with the red wines of the battlefields."*

Easter was a time commemorating sacrifice and resurgence and so the choice of Easter for the Irish insurrection had an added significance. Perhaps the fact that Easter Sunday in 1916 fell on the anniversary of the battle of Clontarf, in which Norse invaders of Ireland had been finally defeated in 1014, made the choice of date for a rising attractive to the romantic-minded. In fact, however, with the serious business of a rising imminent it is doubtful if that date would have been chosen for romantic reasons only. For a number of reasons the insurrection did not take place as planned. It started at noon on Easter Monday. The shock to the bulk of the Irish people was immense. The nobility of spirit of those who took part in it was not immediately recognized.

The poet, AE (George Russell), was to put his reactions into verse: *"Their dream had left me numb and cold,/But yet my spirit rose in pride,/Refashioning in burnished gold/The images of those who died/Or were shut in the penal cell."*

O'DONOVAN ROSSA'S FUNERAL

AFFECTING SCENES IN DUBLIN.

PEARSE DELIVERS SPEECH AT GRAVESIDE.

O'Donovan Rossa's part in the Fenian Rising of '67 and the suffering endured during many years of imprisonment had made his a familiar and honoured name throughout Ireland. His body, which lay in state for three days in the Dublin City Hall, had been brought to Ireland for burial from the United

He was typical of the Irish people, awakened by the glory of the sacrifices made on behalf of Ireland. Yeats might search his conscience: *"Did that play of mine send out/Certain men the English shot?*

Indeed it was not his play, *Cathleen ni Houlihan,* nor even the five plays in which he portrayed Cuchulain, which brought them out; it was rather the general renascence of spirit which had made both them and Yeats what they were.

The spirit which had grown in Ireland in the decades before 1916 was to play a large part in the years which followed. The American poet, Joyce Kilmer, was moved to answer Yeats's poem of 1913: *"Romantic Ireland never dies,/O'Leary lies in fertile ground,/And songs and spears throughout the years/Rise up where patriot graves are found."* He was but echoing the words spoken by Pearse over the grave of the Fenian, O'Donovan Rossa: *"Life springs from death, and from the men and women spring living nations. . . . the fools, the fools, the fools!— they have left us our Fenian dead, and while Ireland holds these graves, Ireland unfree shall never be at peace."* His grave and those of the others who were executed after the Rising were to be the fount of a new inspiration making a new Ireland.□

Padraic Pearse, poet, member of the secret nationalist Irish Republican Brotherhood and moving force in the Volunteers, in his funeral oration exhorted his countrymen to resist British domination. The Volunteers were soon to step up recruitment and training, while the I.R.B. quietly laid plans for armed rebellion.

". . . I propose to you then that, here by the grave of this unrepentant Fenian, we renew our baptismal vows; that, here by the grave of this unconquered and unconquerable man, we ask of God, each one for himself, such unshakable purpose, such high and gallant courage, such unbreakable strength of soul as belonged to O'Donovan Rossa.

"Deliberately here we avow ourselves, as he avowed himself in the dock, Irishmen of one allegiance only. We of the Irish Volunteers, and you others who are associated with us in to-day's task and duty, are bound together and must stand together henceforth in brotherly union for the achievement of the freedom of Ireland. And we know only one definition of freedom; it is Tone's definition; it is Mitchel's definition. It is Rossa's definition. Let no man blaspheme the cause that the dead generations of Ireland served by giving it any other name and definition than their name and their definition.

"We stand at Rossa's grave not in sadness but rather in exaltation of spirit that it has been given to us to come thus into so close a communion with that brave and splendid Gael.... O'Donovan Rossa was splendid in the proud manhood of him, splendid in the heroic grace of him, splendid in the Gaelic strength and clarity and truth of him....

"In a closer spiritual communion with him now than ever before or perhaps ever again, in spiritual communion with those of his day, living and dead, who suffered with him in English prisons, in communion of spirit too with our own dear comrades who suffer in English prisons to-day, and speaking on their behalf as well as our own, we pledge to Ireland our love, and we pledge to English rule in Ireland our hate. This is a place of peace sacred to the dead, where men should speak with all charity and with all restraint; but I hold it a Christian thing, as O'Donovan Rossa held it, to hate evil, to hate untruth, to hate oppression, and hating them, to strive to overthrow them. Our foes are strong and wise and wary; but . . . they cannot undo the miracles of God who ripens in the hearts of young men the seeds sown by the young men of a former generation. And the seeds sown by the young of '65 and '67 are coming to their miraculous ripening to-day. Rulers and Defenders of Realms had need to be wary if they would guard against such processes. Life springs from death: and from the graves of patriot men and women spring living nations. The Defenders of this Realm have worked well in secret and in the open. They think that they have pacified Ireland. They think that they have purchased half of us and intimidated the other half. They think that they have foreseen everything, think that they have provided against everything: but the fools, the fools, the fools!—they have left us our Fenian dead, and while Ireland holds these graves, Ireland unfree shall never be at peace."

— *Padraic Pearse*

*Fearing that disaster was imminent, MacNeill attempted to
call off the maneuvers in an announcement made public
Easter morning. The countermanding order was considerably
effective: only 1200 or so men turned out to parade.*

do not propose to remain schoolboys for ever.

I have often said (quoting, I think, Herbert Spencer) that education should be a preparation for complete living; and I say now that our Gaelic League education ought to have been a preparation for our complete living as Irish Nationalists. In proportion as we have been faithful and diligent Gaelic Leaguers, our work as Irish Nationalists (by which term I mean people who accept the ideal of, and work for, the realisation of an Irish Nation, by whatever means) will be earnest and thorough, a valiant and worthy fighting, not the mere carrying out of a ritual. As to what your work as an Irish Nationalist is to be, I cannot conjecture; I know what mine is to be, and would have you know yours and buckle yourself to it. And it may be (nay, it is) that yours and mine will lead us to a common meeting-place, and that on a certain day we shall stand together, with many more beside us, ready for a greater adventure than any of us has yet had, a trial and a triumph to be endured and achieved in common.

This is what I meant when I said that our work henceforward must be done less and less through the Gaelic League and more and more through the groups and the individuals that have arisen, or are arising, out of the Gaelic League. There will be in the Ireland of the next few years a multitudinous

NO PARADES!

Irish Volunteer Marches Cancelled

A SUDDEN ORDER.

April 22, 1916.
Owing to the very critical position, all orders given to Irish Volunteers for tomorrow, Easter Sunday, are hereby rescinded, and no

activity of Freedom Clubs, Young Republican Parties, Labour Organisations, Socialist Groups, and what not; bewildering enterprises undertaken by sane persons and insane persons, by good men and bad men, many of them seemingly contradictory, some mutually destructive, yet all of them tending towards a common objective, and that objective: the Irish Revolution.

For if there is one thing that has become plainer than another it is that when the seven men met in O'Connell Street to found the Gaelic League, they were commencing, had there been a Liancourt there to make the epigram, not a revolt, but a revolution. The work of the Gaelic League, its appointed work, was that; and the work is done. To every generation its deed. The deed of the generation that has now reached middle life was the Gaelic League, the beginning of the Irish Revolution. Let our generation not shirk *its* deed, which is to accomplish the revolution.

I believe that the national movement of which the Gaelic League has been the soul has reached the point which O'Connell's movement had reached at the close of the series of monster meetings. Indeed, I believe that our movement reached that point a few years ago—say, at the conclusion of the fight for Essential Irish; and I said so at the time. The moment was *(Continued on page 54)*

(Left) The General Post Office Building, Dublin (with columns), soon to become general headquarters of the Provisional Government of the Irish Republic. In the foreground is O'Connell Street.

*Little attention was paid to the marching of the Citizen Army and
Volunteers on Easter Monday. By the time the populace was
aware that the "invasions" into public buildings were no longer
the mock attacks they had become accustomed to, the G.P.O.
had been occupied by forces of the Republic . . .*

*. . . Later in that day a new tri-color flag was hoisted over the
Post Office, while on its steps Padraic Pearse read the
official proclamation claiming authority for the
Provisional Government of the Irish Republic.*

*As Republicans fortified the occupied buildings and
improvised barricades, the British in Dublin
called for military reinforcement.*

(Top) British soldiers behind barricade.
(Bottom) Armored truck, built by the underequipped British in eight hours in a Dublin engineering yard.

Facsimile of the Insurgent Newspaper. Only this single issue was published.

IRISH WAR NEWS

THE IRISH REPUBLIC.

VOL. 1. No. 1   DUBLIN, TUESDAY, APRIL 25, 1916.   ONE PENNY

"IF THE GERMANS CONQUERED ENGLAND."

In the London "New Statesman" for *April 1st*, an article is published—"If the Germans Conquered England," which has the appearance of a very clever piece of satire written by an Irishman. The writer draws a picture of England under German rule, almost every detail of which exactly fits the case of Ireland at the present day. Some of the sentences are so exquisitely appropriate that it is impossible to believe that the writer had not Ireland in his mind when he wrote them. For instance :—

"England would be constantly irritated by the lofty moral utterances of German statesmen who would assert—quite sincerely, no doubt—that England was free, freer indeed than she had ever been before. Prussian freedom, they would explain, was the only real freedom, and therefore England was free. They would point to the flourishing railways and farms and colleges. They would possibly point to the contingent of M.P.'s, which was permitted, in spite of its deplorable disorderliness, to sit in a permanent minority in the Reich-

stag. And not only would the Englishman have to listen to a constant flow of speeches of this sort ; he would find a respectable official Press secret bought over by the Government to say the same kind of things over and over, every day of the week. He would find, too, that his children were coming home from school with new ideas of history. . . They would ask him if it was true that until the Germans came England had been an unruly country, constantly engaged in civil war. . . . The object of every schoolbook would be to make the English child grow up in the notion that the history of his country was a thing to forget, and that the one bright spot in it was the fact that it had been conquered by cultured Germany.'

"If there was a revolt, German statesmen would deliver grave speeches about "disloyalty," "ingratitude," "reckless agitators who would ruin their country's prosperity. . . . Prussian soldiers would be encamped in every barracks—the English conscripts having been sent out of the country to be trained in Germany, or to fight the Chinese—in order to come to the aid of German morality, should English sedition come to blows with it."

"England would be exhorted to abandon her own genius in order to imitate the genius of her conquerors, to forget her own history for a larger history, to give up her own language for a " universal" language—in other words, to destroy her household gods one by one, and put in their place alien gods. Such an England would be an England without a soul, without even a mind. She would be a nation of slaves, even though every slave in the country had a chicken in his pot and a golden dish to serve it on."

Put "Ireland" in the place of "England" in these extracts and "England" in the place of "Germany," and it will be admitted that the humiliating state of national subjection in which we live, and the cunning methods of spiritual conquest practised on us by England have seldom been better described. If the article was not written by an Irishman in a bitterly satiric mood, it shows how well Englishmen understand how the treatment they have been accustomed to apply to other nations would feel, applied to themselves. But my own opinion certainly is, that every sentence I have quoted stamps the article as the production of a very able Sinn Féiner.

❖

THEN AND NOW

If there is one personality which the canting hypocracy of England is using more than another to play upon the religious susceptibilities of Catholics it is Cardinal Mercier. The British press and its Irish jackals are watching for everything that may give them a chance of using the Cardinal's name in a manner prejudicial to German methods. The British Government exploited him through London, and the saintly T. P. O'Connor, who has prostituted every religious and Nationalist principle he ever held, took the Cardinal under his Masonic wing, and, on introducing him to an audience, was moved to tears—truly, the greatest miracle in water since Moses struck the rock. One of the things that has struck most of us in connection with this exploiting of Belgium and her Cardinal by the British Press and politicians, is what must be the real honest opinion of the Belgians and his Eminence on this new-found friendship for their country.

We remember at the time of the death of King Leopold of Belgium, what an unholy lust these same politicians displayed for the grabbing of Belgium's territory, and to what depths of scurrilous mendacity they descended to belie the mora-character of the country which they had hoped to plunder. Alfred Morce, and the other mainsprings, stirred up the agitation for English intervention in the Congo, as the only hope for saving the hands and heads of the natives from being cut off. English influence showed its power in manipulating the Press Agencies to prejudice world feeling against the Belgians. King Leopold was not cold in his grave when his private affairs and morals were laid bare to the gaze of the curious, and this kind of thing, with the usual garnish of pruriency, was served up *ad nauseam*. Had they wished the Belgians might have met this stirring up of stagnant streams by reminding the English of another Royal personage and a trip to Scarborough, and a cruise to India, which would not stand the light of day, according to the accepted standards of morality, but the Belgians though smarting under the indignities heaped upon them and their dead monarch, ignored "the war of filth," as one French newspaper called this British subsidized scandal-mongering.

A protest signed by all the leaders of political and religious thought in Belgium was sent to Washington for presentation to Congress. Cardinal Mercier appended his name as a protest against the foul-mouthed British libels on his country. So did Mons. Beernaert, President of the Executive Council, and other Ministers of State; Dr. Rochedier, President of the Synod of Evangelical Protestant Churches. Dr. Bioch, Chief Rabbi; the Presidents of the House of Representatives, the Senate of the Supreme Court, the Court of Appeals, the Royal Academy, and all other important bodies.

That is not so long ago, and Belgium cannot be unmindful of the campaign of calumny which such hired ink-slingers as Alfred Morel, Sir Conan Doyle, Stackpole, and the lesser fry carried on "to save humanity from Belgium barbarities," and incidentally, of course, handed over the Congo to the British Rubber monopolists. Belgium is in its present position as the result of a weak King, for Alfred has none of the strength which his father displayed in keeping out of the meashes spread by British intrigue. British intrigue has made a cat's-paw of Belgium in this affair, and as a result the once prosperous little Kingdom is to-day shattered and broken. Britain has paraded her before the world, and begged some money for her from the charitable of all nations, and to-day, through her press and her press agencies, she calls on God and the world to witness what has been done for "destitute Belgium" by the power of "British benevolence."

A CHANGE OF FRONT

"N.D." writing in the orthodox "Frontier Sentinel" (Newry), puts the Parliamentarian attitude towards the Irish Volunteers in a new and almost hitherto unheard of light. Referring to the famous Banishment Orders, he says :—

Not less odious than the attempt to disarm the MacNeill Volunteers is the attempt to banish the organisers—a prelude, I suppose, to the intended total disruption of the organisation. It is, of course, a policy which will never achieve success. It would be bad enough if this were the work of a native Parliament, but words are inadequate to describe its enormity when we consider it is engineered from Dublin Castle—that strange, undefinable thing, that stole Red Hugh O'Donnell away from the people, that in Cromwell's days, sent the best blood of the nation to the horrors of the Barbadoes, that banished the priests and the schoolmasters ; the thing that has the blood of the United Irishmen leaders on it, sent Mitchel and his associates to the hulks, paid to the informers against the Fenians the price of their perfidy ; plotted the downfall of Parnell, used all its cunning and cruelty against the Land League, and told the police : "Do not hesitate to shoot." If this is the thing that the followers of Mr. Mac Neill are being made the victims of, then I say, though I absolutely abhor and reprobate their policy, that they are being honoured beyond their deserts. If the bitterest Orangeman that ever breathed were victimised by the stupid anachronism of Dublin Castle, to use an expression of the late Joseph Chamberlain, I should be proud to have his acquaintance. Those who have decreed the banishment of these men are reckoning without their host. Ireland has already condemned "senseless prosecutions," and the deportation of Irishmen who, at the worst, can only be described as political oddities ; and it will continue to voice its indignation. The powers of a national government—even of an autocratic and stupid government—must not be usurped by anybody else, be he benevolent or autocratic, intelligent or stupid. What Dublin Castle needs, and what it never had, is a sense of humour. That is its own business, however. What we Nationalists want is not only to keep ourselves clear from the imputation that we are in any way responsible for the "Realm Act" policy that is being adopted against the Irish Volunteers, but to show that we completely disapprove of it. We have already done so, and we must continue. Ridiculous as the MacNeillites are, they stand for a principle that all Home Rulers have irrevocably adopted—the principle of an armed force responsible to an Irish Government ; and, after all, principles are more sacred than personalities.

Under the caption "Manufacturing Sinn Feiners" "N.D." continues to strike a new note.

We know the story of the English farmer, who finding a toad on the roadside, began to beat it with a stick, saying : "Ah, you toad ! I will teach you to be a toad." So, in pursuing a policy of uncompromising hostility towards the Irish Volunteers I consider that we are not only further antagonising the Sinn Fein element amongst them, but driving into the ranks of Sinn Feinism those members who have merely joined out of the conviction that it is the inalienable right of the Irish people to bear arms in self-defence. That is a right which has been declared from thousands of platforms of all shades of opinion in Ireland, and anybody who is opposed to it cannot claim to be a Nationalist. Instead of manufacturing Sinn Feiners by referring to the MacNeill following as "The Irish Volunteers"—an organisation which has no existence, so far as I know—would it not be better to endeavour to show those people the error of their ways and behave towards them in as charitable a manner, at least, as we have behaved towards the Carsonite opponents of Home Rule, who but a short time ago were threatening Nationalists (meaning Irish Catholics) with bloody war ? God forgive me if I am wrong, but I hold it to be proper to treat all Irishmen, no matter what their religious or political views may be, with respect, and when we feel obliged to oppose their policies to do so with clean weapons and not with those of misrepresentation and abuse.

THINGS THEY OUGHT TO TAX

The British Exchequer appears to be hard up. Why not tax the following sources of revenue :—

Resolutions of Confidence in the "Party."

Licences permitting "Party" orators the indiscriminate use of opprobrious terms, such as "cranks," "soreheads," "factionists," etc.

Molly Maguire Lodges, and similar insanitary buildings.

Mr. Justice Kenny's "Alarms and excursions" addresses to Dublin Juries.

Public bodies who wish to change their minds about taxation and other bogies.

STOP PRESS!

THE IRISH REPUBLIC

(Irish) "War News" is published to-day because a momentous thing has happened. The Irish Republic has been declared in Dublin, and a Provisional Government has been appointed to adminster its affairs. The following have been named as the Provisional Government :—

> Thomas J. Clarke.
> Sean Mac Diarmada
> P. H. Pearse.
> James Connolly.
> Thomas Mac Donagh.
> Eamonn Ceannt.
> Joseph Plunkett.

The Irish Republic was proclaimed by a poster, which was prominently displayed in Dublin.

At 9.30 a.m. this morning the following statement was made by Commandant-General, P. H. Pearse :—

The Irish Republic was proclaimed in Dublin on Easter Monday, 24th April, at 12 noon. Simultaneously with the issue of the proclamation of the Provisional Government the Dublin Division of the Army of the Republic, including the Irish Volunteers, Citizen Army, Hibernian Rifles, and other bodies, occupied dominating points in the city. The G.P.O. was seized at 12 noon, the Castle was attacked at the same moment, and shortly afterwards the Four Courts were oecupied. The Irish troops hold the City Hall and dominate the Castle. Attacks were immediately commenced by the British forces and were everywhere repulsed. At the moment of writing this report, (9.30 a.m., Tuesday) the Republican forces hold all their positions and the British forces have nowhere broken through. There has been heavy and continuous fighting for nearly 24 hours, the casualties of the enemy being much more numerous than those on the Republican side. The Republican forces everywhere are fighting with splendid gallantry. The populace of Dublin are plainly with the Republic, and the officers and men are everywhere cheered as they march through the streets. The whole centre of the city is in the hands of the Republic, whose flag flies from the G.P.O.

Commandant General P. H. Pearse is commanding in chief of the Army of the Republic and is President of the Provisional Government Commandant General James Connolly is commanding the Dublin districts. Communication with the country is largely cut, but reports to hand show that the country is rising, and bodies of men from Kildare and Fingall have already reported in Dublin.

MORE PIRACY.

The condition of affairs illustrated in the following comment from " The Advocate," a New York Irish Redmondite paper, is not at all unlike piracy on the high seas. In its latest issue to hand " The Advocate " says :—

"Since the British Government began to seize the mails we have been informed by some of our Swedish acquaintances that the little cheques they have sent to the old folks at home have never reached their destination. If this be true, and we have no reason to doubt it, then the British Government stands convicted of the most contemptible kind of petty larceny which the criminal annals of the world can show. Sweden is just now experiencing a depression in all kinds of business owing to being cut off from other neutral nations by Great Britain, and consequently a little help from their exiled brethren is much needed in countless Swedish households. Now, it may be asked what Great Britain hopes to accomplish by preventing the exiled Swedes from helping their suffering kindred at home ? The reason is not far to seek. The Socialist party is very strong in Sweden, and is growing stronger in proportion to the increase in the difficulty of the masses to make ends meet. Now, Great Britain knows that were it not for the opposition of the Socialists Sweden would long since have entered the war on the side of Germany, hence it is to her interest to add by every means at her disposal to the Socialists' power. Therefore in robbing the mails of these little cheques she is robbing deserving people of the means of tiding over the dull season, and expects that, driven by necessity, many will turn to the Socialists in their extremity, and thus Sweden's continued neutrality will be secured. This is the explanation our Swedish acquaintances give of England's thieving conduct in this regard. For the honour of our poor human nature, let us hope the case is not as bad as it is said to be."

By the second day of the Rising, Tuesday, British artillery was being brought into action. Meanwhile, small groups of Irish Volunteers from the country were coming to Dublin to join their comrades. They were shortly to find it impossible to make contact with Republican positions.

Arms and ámmunition being rushed to Dublin from Howth.

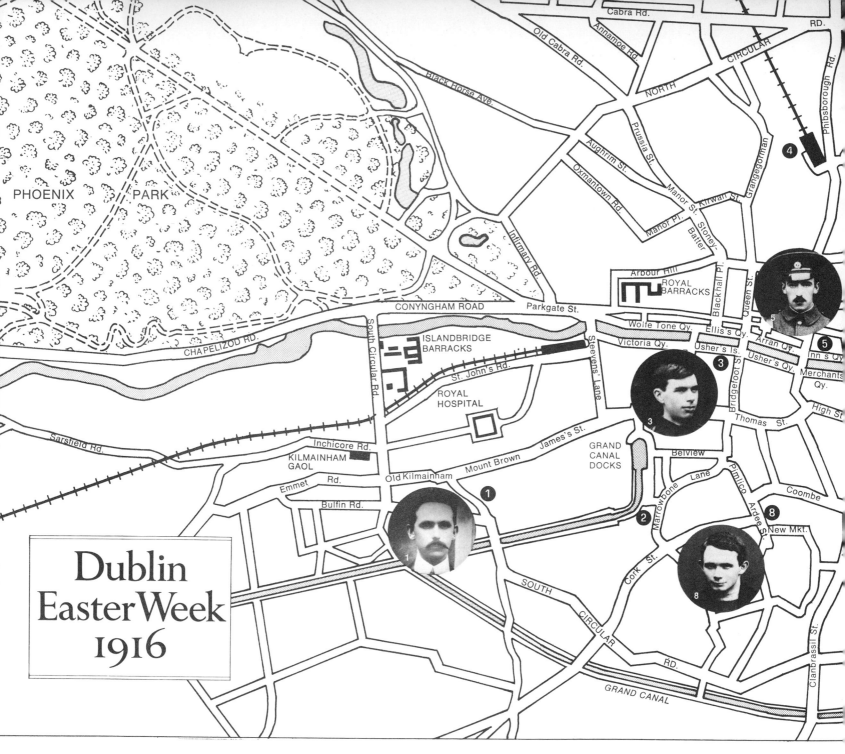

Dublin Easter Week 1916

1. So. Dublin Union: Under the command of Eamonn Ceannt (photo) this position—vital for its proximity to British HQ in Royal Hospital—was held by hand-to-hand combat till the Surrender.

2. Marrowbone Lane Distillery

3. Mendicity Institute: Sean Heuston (photo) and 23 men captured position to delay passage of British on north quays.

They were ordered to hold for 3 or 4 hours, and held instead for 3 days.

4. Broadstone Railway Terminus

5. Four Courts: Under Edward Daly (photo) company destroyed Army Pay Center and captured British garrison. After heavy fighting, position was surrounded.

6. Dublin Castle

7. Portobello Bridge

8. Watkins Distillery: Con Colbert (photo) was unable to hold with 15 men, and joined the group at Marrowbone La. Distillery.

9. Dublin City Hall: Sean Connolly (photo) took to contain British in Dublin Castle across the way. Position given up after heavy bombardment, entire company surrendered, and Connolly killed.

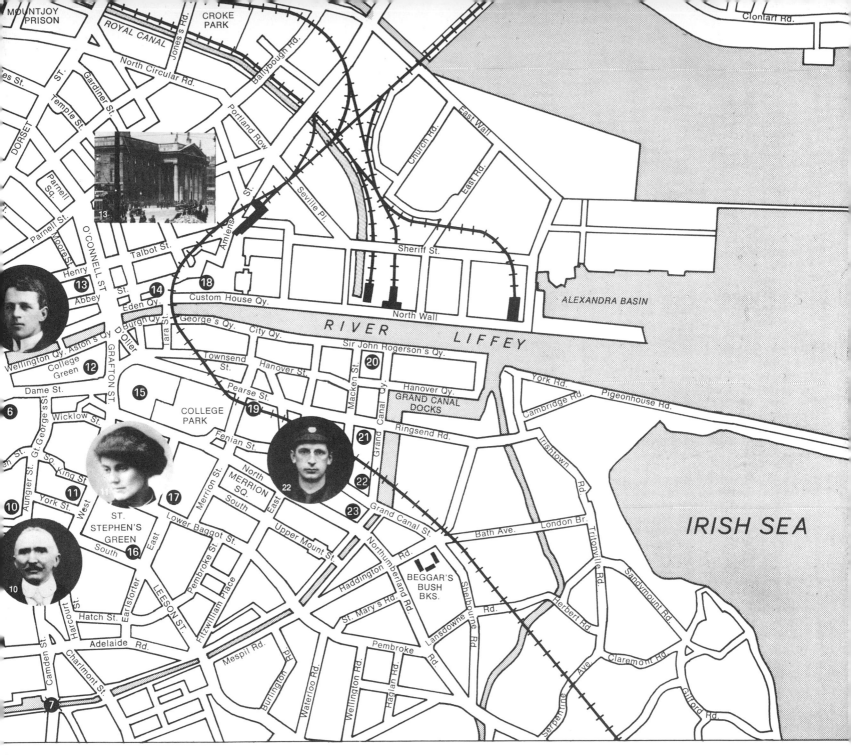

10. Jacob's Factory: Sean MacBride (photo) and Thomas MacDonagh led group using factory's towers as a vantage point for sniping.

11. College of Surgeons: Countess Markievicz (photo) took and held this position, commanding St. Stephen's Green, with fighting intermittent but costly.

12. Bank of Ireland

13. Post Office (photo): HQ of Provisional Gov't and signers of the Proclamation, set on fire and gutted by the British.

14. Liberty Hall

15. Trinity College

16. St. Stephen's Green

17. Shelbourne Hotel

18. Custom House

19. Westland Row Railway Station

20. Gas Co.

21. Hammond Lane Foundry

22. Boland's Mills: Eamon de Valera (photo) commanded 5 companies with main objective of cutting British supply route on railway line through area. Fighting was extremely heavy, casualties high.

23. Clanwilliam House

During the week that followed, position after position held by
Republicans was given up to the British. Connolly was wounded,
the Post Office burning, and on Friday morning Pearse issued a
statement renouncing hope of military success.

(Right) Behind the barricade in the Four Courts.

The hoped-for Rising in the countryside failed to materialize;
the new Republic would be left to stand or fall with Dublin,
and by Friday afternoon Pearse was forced to
evacuate the Post Office.

Scenes of the extensive damage brought upon Dublin during Easter Week.

Children carrying wood from O'Connell Street.

British soldiers inspect the remains of the Post Office Building.

The decision to surrender was reached on Saturday morning.
The British demanded that the surrender be unconditional,
and at half-past three Pearse surrendered his sword to
Brigadier General Lowe.

(Right) Eamon de Valera under armed escort after his surrender.

[44]

The men from Boland Mills district marching in to surrender their arms. X indicates their commander, Eamon de Valera.

*At 9:00 in the evening, the men from Moore Street headquarters
marched in silence up O'Connell Street and threw down their
arms before the statue of Parnell. During the next day the
remaining outposts in the city, though not without some
resistance, followed suit . . .*

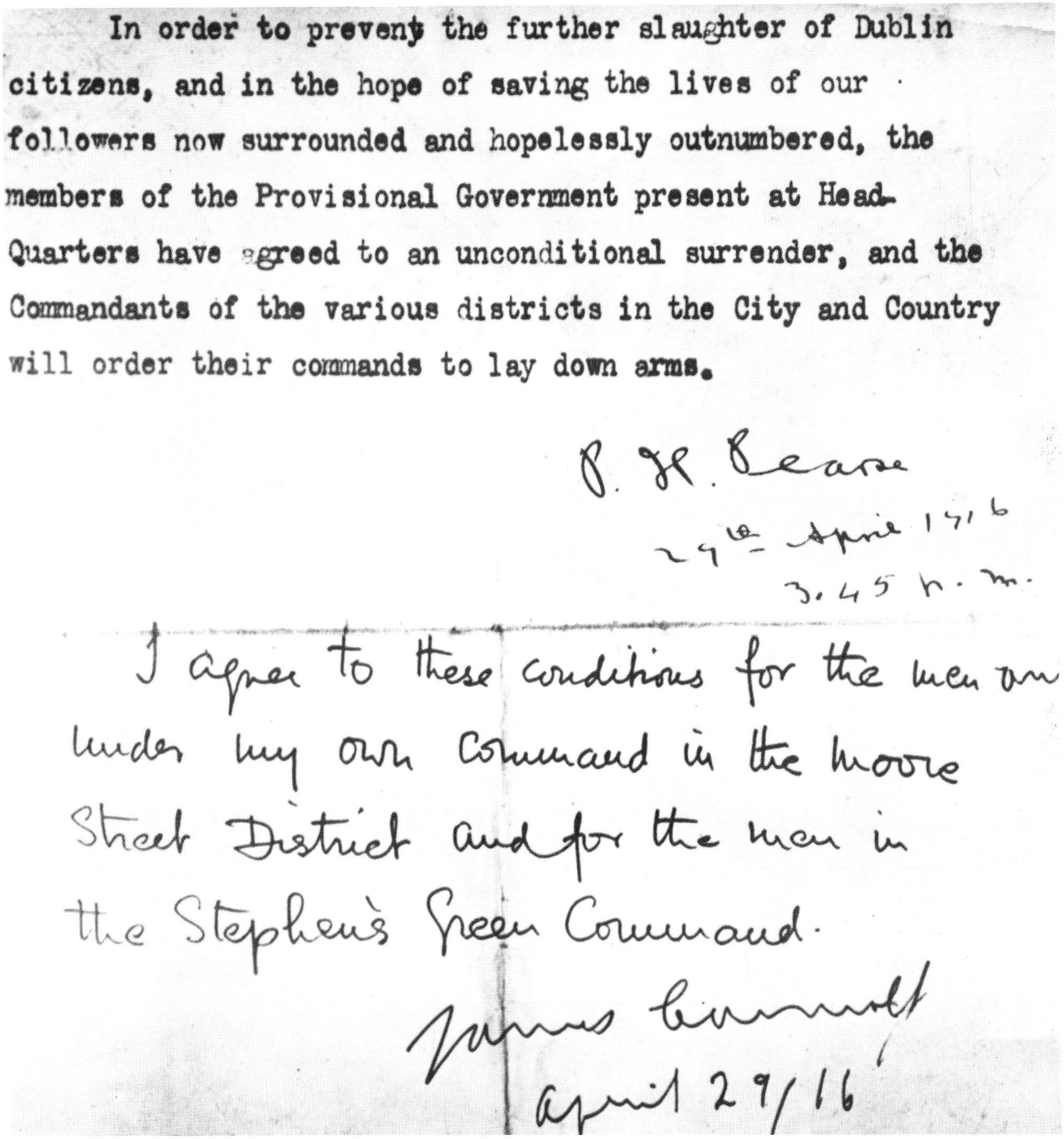

In order to prevent the further slaughter of Dublin
citizens, and in the hope of saving the lives of our
followers now surrounded and hopelessly outnumbered, the
members of the Provisional Government present at Head-
Quarters have agreed to an unconditional surrender, and the
Commandants of the various districts in the City and Country
will order their commands to lay down arms.

P. H. Pearse

29th April 1916
3.45 p. m.

*I agree to these conditions for the men on
under my own Command in the Moore
Street District and for the men in
the Stephen's Green Command.*

James Connolly

April 29/16

The surrender order, dated April 29, 1916, 3:45 P.M., issued by Pearse and countersigned by James Connolly.

. . . and the Rising of Easter Week was over. The British
estimated that 56 volunteers had been killed in action and that
the total number of casualties during the week had been
a little over 3000.

Aftermath of the Uprising: (Top) British soldiers patrol Dublin streets (Bottom) Prisoners being escorted to jail.

(Right) The remains of the Imperial Hotel.

O'Connell Street after the Rising.

COLLAPSE OF THE SINN FEIN REVOLT.

ROUNDING UP THE REBELS.

SCENES OF DEVASTATION IN DUBLIN.

HAVOC IN SACKVILLE STREET.

The information received in official quarters yesterday was to the effect that the rebels are surrendering throughout the country. They have surrendered at Enniscorthy.

At Ashbourne, County Meath, where nine police constables and District Inspector Smith were killed, and County Inspector Gray and fourteen constables were wounded in disturbances which occurred there, all is now quiet.

Arrangements are in process of completion for the reopening of traffic on the railways, and also for establishing a temporary General Post Office in Dublin.

In Galway, where disturbances threatened to develop, surrenders are taking place.

The Revolution of the Sinn Feiners of Dublin having ended in the unconditional surrender of almost the entire army of rebels, and the streets in the central parts of the city having become comparatively safe during daylight, the citizens displayed great anxiety to see for themselves some of the damage that had been done. Residents outside the military cordon on the North side of the city were rigorously excluded from passing through, and on the South side a similar restriction, but not quite so strict, was in force. Those who lived within the cordon were in no way hindered from moving about and viewing the wreck of their once fine city. The spectators appeared as if spellbound when they came into view of Sackville street. Here and there a cloud of smoke rose from a smouldering ruin. Only a few blackened walls remain of the whole range of business houses on one side of the street between Nelson's Pillar and O'Connell Bridge, if the shell of Clery's warehouse is excepted. On the other side of the street only the outer walls and the portico of the General Post Office remain, the Hotel Metropole is gone, and most of the other business places from that point down to O'Connell Bridge are either partially or wholly destroyed.

A TERRIBLE PERIL.

As if not content with the ruin they had brought upon the city, the rebels had in contemplation a plan of destruction appalling to contemplate. By some means at present unknown they had concealed at the back of the General Post Office a very large quantity of dynamite and other powerful explosives. Fortunately the military authorities got to know of the presence of this terrible danger while the postal building was in flames, and the soldiers and firemen, with a courage worthy of the highest commendation, put forth every

tions of street fighting, which it was found necessary to order, were thanked for their splendid behaviour. He specially mentions with gratitude those Irish regiments "who have so largely helped to crush this rising."

JAMES CONNOLLY A PRISONER.

It is understood that James Connolly, the rebel leader, who was wounded in the General Post Office and taken prisoner, is seriously, but not dangerously, hurt. He was shot through the femur of the right leg.

Connolly succeeded James Larkin as secretary of the Transport Workers' Union and organiser of the "Citizen Army." He was one of the seven signatories of the declaration of "the Provisional Government of the Irish Republic." The others are—Thomas J. Clarke, Sean Mac Diarmada, Thomas Mac-Donagh, P. H. Pearse, Eamonn Ceannt, and Joseph Plunkett.

JACOB'S FACTORY.

The surrender of the Volunteers who occupied Jacob's Factory took place on Sunday afternoon. It was a member of the Carmelite Order from Whitefriar street who was instrumental in persuading them to yield. Amid the cheers of the crowd gathered about the building, the clergyman was hoisted by a number of men up to one of the lower windows, from which the bags of flour used instead of sand by the rebels had been pulled. He went inside the factory, and not long after a party of Volunteers walked out.

REBELS AT CORK.

HOW THE RISING FAILED.

A correspondent at Cork reports an interview with the leader of a body of Sinn Fein

OFFICIAL REPORTS.

THE UNCONDITIONAL SURRENDER.

REPORTS FROM VISCOUNT FRENCH.

From Field-Marshal Viscount French, Commanding-in-Chief Home Forces:
Dublin, Saturday Night.

Dublin.—The situation this morning had improved considerably, but the rebels were still offering serious resistance in the neighbourhood of Sackville street.

The cordon of troops encircling this quarter was, however, steadily closing in, but the house-to-house fighting necessarily rendered this progress slow. The Post Office and a block of buildings east of Sackville street have been destroyed by fire. A party of rebels have been driven out of Boland's mills, Ringsend, by guns mounted on motor lorries.

One of the rebel leaders, a man named Pearse, was said to be in this area, and was wounded in the leg. A report received this evening states that Pearse has surrendered unconditionally, and that he asserts he has authority to accept the same terms of surrender for his followers in Dublin.

Another leader, James Connolly, is reported killed.

The Four Courts district, which is still held by the rebels, is also surrounded by a cordon of troops, which is gradually closing in.

All the information to hand points to the conclusion that the rebellion, so far as Dublin is concerned, is on the verge of collapse. A considerable number of rebels are prisoners in military custody.

OTHER OUTBREAKS.

Reports received this evening from the rest of Ireland are generally satisfactory. The conditions in Belfast and the Ulster Province are normal, and the situation in Londonderry is stated to be quite satisfactory.

The district within fifteen miles of Galway is also reported to be normal, but a band of rebels has been located between Athenry and Craughwell.

Nineteen rebel prisoners have been captured and are on their way to Queenstown.

Another band of rebels are reported to have entrenched themselves at Enniscorthy, but the police are still holding out, and the roads and railways are clear to within four miles of the town.

The damage to the Barrow bridge on the Dublin and South-Eastern Railway, is now reported not to be serious.

SUNDAY'S REPORT.

From the Field-Marshal Commanding-in-Chief Home Forces:—
Sunday, 6.45 p.m.
The General Officer Commanding-in-

A GENERAL SHORTAG

RELIEF MEASURES.

THE CRISIS PASSED.

The rebellion created a grave prob every home—how to refill the larder rebels had hardly been a day at the work when food supplies began to run The baker, the grocer, the milkman, a butcher sent their goods as usual on T in most districts, but then when began to develop, and when commun between the city and suburbs was c supplies quickly diminished. As the grew older food became scarcer, an worries of the householder increased ingly. The baker's cart did not the front door, because it had been h and its load of loaves quickly sold to purchasers. The butcher was almost meat, and the grocer could hardly me demands of his customers. The price of was doubled, trebled, and in one inst least seven and sixpence per lb. was When butter could no longer be pro margarine was sought as a substitute, Saturday the supply was almost exha As much as half-a-crown per stone wa for potatoes. Bread was extremely sca through the week, owing to the fact th of the principal bakeries in the city, t Messrs. Boland, was in the hands rebels.

ABNORMAL DEMANDS.

Other bakeries were consequently upon to make special efforts to cope w situation, and their several staffs d every credit for the efforts which they to meet the abnormal demands upon the put. Flour and meal were virtuall out early in the week, and by Satur some instances, four shillings and te was demanded for a stone of flour. M increased in price by a shilling per several shops, but the better class t increased their prices only by fourpen lb. Vegetables were almost unprocura several days, until it became known surrounding districts that high prices to be obtained by bringing supplies in city. When it was ascertained that s were forthcoming, prices were quick stored almost to their usual scale. In outlying suburbs fields of cabbage and flower, the property of large market deners, were entered by gangs of poor who liberally helped themselves to a pl supply, owing to the scarcity of brea meat. The milk supply failed in som tricts, with the result that there was a g demand for condensed milk. Towar end of the week eggs were unprocurabl demands of the military, which were na increased owing to the large increase number of soldiers in the city, contribu the scarcity of food. Traders and the generally, of course, recognised that the fenders had first call upon the supplie they willingly gave precedence to the mands. The authorities, however, pr that immediate facilities would be af for replenishing the stocks of the tr

NOVEL SCENES.

The rush for food was such an imp matter, and the means of delivery w greatly impeded, that people pocketed pride and went forraging for themselves amusing scenes were witnessed, and it novel sight to see well-known clergymen fessional and commercial men, passing struggling with bundles of cauliflowers bage, meat, biscuits, bread, and a th and one other articles, which in or times would be sent home in receptacle imposing than a wrapping of old newsp

Police and military now set out to arrest known nationalists
all over Ireland. Irish opinion, largely apathetic about the Rising,
stirred at the news that the British Commander-in-Chief,
General Sir John Maxwell, had ordered the execution
of the surrendered leaders.

British officers posing with the captured flag of the Irish Republic.

*The executions, carried out after a series of secret courts martial,
began on May 3rd. Within two weeks fifteen men were to be shot.
Sixty-five others were transported to England for life imprisonment.*

ripe then for a new Young Ireland Party, with a forward policy; and we have lost much by our hesitation. I propose in all seriousness that we hesitate no longer—that we push on. I propose that we leave Conciliation Hall behind us and go into the Irish Confederation.

Whenever Dr. Hyde, at a meeting at which I have had a chance of speaking after him, has produced his dove of peace, I have always been careful to produce my sword; and to tantalise him by saying that the Gaelic League has brought into Ireland "Not Peace, but a Sword." But this does not show any fundamental difference of outlook between my leader and me; for while he is thinking of peace between brother-Irishmen, I am thinking of the sword-point between banded Irishmen and the foreign force that occupies Ireland, and his peace is necessary to my war. It is evident that there can be no peace between the body politic and a foreign substance that has intruded itself into its system; between them war only until the foreign substance is expelled or assimilated.

Whether Home Rule means a loosening or a tightening of England's grip upon Ireland remains yet to be seen. But the coming of Home Rule, if come it does, will make no material difference in the nature of the work that lies before us; it will affect only the means we are to employ, our plan

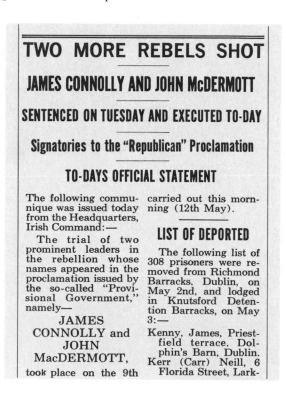

TWO MORE REBELS SHOT

JAMES CONNOLLY AND JOHN McDERMOTT

SENTENCED ON TUESDAY AND EXECUTED TO-DAY

Signatories to the "Republican" Proclamation

TO-DAYS OFFICIAL STATEMENT

The following communique was issued today from the Headquarters, Irish Command:—

The trial of two prominent leaders in the rebellion whose names appeared in the proclamation issued by the so-called "Provisional Government," namely—

JAMES CONNOLLY and **JOHN MacDERMOTT,** took place on the 9th

carried out this morning (12th May).

LIST OF DEPORTED

The following list of 308 prisoners were removed from Richmond Barracks, Dublin, on May 2nd, and lodged in Knutsford Detention Barracks, on May 3:—

Kenny, James, Priestfield terrace, Dolphin's Barn, Dublin. Kerr (Carr) Neill, 6 Florida Street, Lark-

of campaign. There remains, under Home Rule as in its absence, the substantial task of achieving the Irish Nation.

I do not think it is going to be achieved without stress and trial, without suffering and bloodshed; at any rate, it is not going to be achieved without *work*. Our business here and now is to get ourselves into harness for such work as has to be done.

I hold that before we can do any work, any *men's* work, we must first realise ourselves as men. Whatever comes to Ireland, she needs men. And we of this generation are not in any real sense men; for we suffer things that men do not suffer, and we seek to redress grievances by means which men do not employ. We have, for instance, allowed ourselves to be disarmed; and, now that we have the chance of re-arming, we are not seizing it. Professor Eoin MacNeill pointed out last week that we have at this moment an opportunity of rectifying the capital error we made when we allowed ourselves to be disarmed; and such opportunities, he reminds us, do not always come back to nations.

A thing that stands demonstrable is that nationhood is not achieved otherwise than in arms: in one or two instances there may have been no actual bloodshed, but the arms were there and the ability to use them. Ireland unarmed will attain just as

"Grass soon grows over the battlefield but never over the scaffold."
It has been said that in the yard of Kilmainham jail (below),
where the fifteen were executed, the British insured the success
of an otherwise hapless Rising. The dead men, before considered
madmen at best, were now national heroes.

much freedom as it is convenient for England to give her; Ireland armed will attain ultimately just as much freedom as she wants. These are matters which may not concern the Gaelic League, as a body; but they concern every member of the Gaelic League, and every man and woman of Ireland. I urged much of this five or six years ago in addresses to the Ard-Chraobh:[1] but the League was too busy with resolutions to think of revolution, and the only resolution that a member of the League could not come to was the resolution to be a man. My fellow-Leaguers had not (and have not) apprehended that the thing which cannot defend itself, even though it wear trousers, is no man.

I am glad, then, that the North has "begun." I am glad that the Orangemen have armed, for it is a goodly thing to see arms in Irish hands. I should like to see the A.O.H.[2] armed. I should like to see the Transport Workers armed. I should like to see any and every body of Irish citizens armed. We must accustom ourselves to the thought of arms, to the sight of arms, to the use of arms. We may make mistakes in the beginning and shoot the wrong people; but bloodshed is a cleansing and a sanctifying thing, and the nation which regards it as the final horror has lost its manhood. There are many things more horrible than bloodshed; and slavery is one of them. □

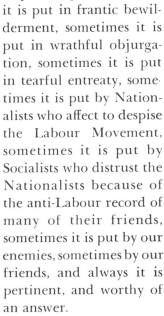

II. What Is Our Programme?[3]
by James Connolly

JANUARY 1916

WE ARE often asked the above question. Sometimes the question is not too politely put, sometimes it is put in frantic bewilderment, sometimes it is put in wrathful objurgation, sometimes it is put in tearful entreaty, sometimes it is put by Nationalists who affect to despise the Labour Movement, sometimes it is put by Socialists who distrust the Nationalists because of the anti-Labour record of many of their friends, sometimes it is put by our enemies, sometimes by our friends, and always it is pertinent, and worthy of an answer.

The Labour Movement is like no other movement. Its strength lies in being like no other movement. It is never so strong as when it stands alone. Other movements dread analysis and shun all attempts to define their objects. The Labour Movement delights in analysing, and is perpetually defining and re-defining its principles and objects.

The man or woman who has caught the spirit of the Labour Movement brings that spirit of analysis and definition into all his *(Continued on page 61)*

---

1 The governing body of the Gaelic League.
2 Ancient Order of Hibernians.

3 From *The Workers' Republic*, Vol. I, No. 35, Dublin, January 22, 1916.

Padraic Pearse

Thomas MacDonagh

Thomas Clarke

Joseph Mary Plunkett

Michael O'Hanrahan

Edward Daly

William Pearse

Sean MacBride

Sean Heuston

Eamonn Ceannt

Michael Mallin

Cornelius Colbert

Sean MacDermott

James Connolly

Thomas Kent

Roger Casement

*The British had called for a convention of Irish representatives
which was to meet in Dublin in July, 1917, and recommend
some settlement of Ireland's future. To ease the unfavorable
atmosphere surrounding the convention, the Sinn Fein prisoners
were pardoned from life sentences and returned home.*

or her public acts, and expects at all times to answer the call to define their position. They cannot live on illusions, nor thrive by them; even should their heads be in the clouds they will make no forward step until they are assured that their feet rest upon the solid earth.

In this they are essentially different from the middle or professional classes, and the parties or movements controlled by such classes in Ireland. These always talk of realities, but nourish themselves and their followers upon the unsubstantial meat of phrases; always prate about being intensely practical but nevertheless spend their whole lives in following visions.

When the average non-Labour patriot in Ireland who boasts of his practicality is brought in contact with the cold world and its problems he shrinks from the contact, should his feet touch the solid earth he affects to despise it as a "mere material basis," and strives to make the people believe that true patriotism needs no foundation to rest upon other than the brainstorms of its poets, orators, journalists, and leaders.

Ask such people for a programme and you are branded as a carping critic; refuse to accept their judgment as the last word in human wisdom and you become an enemy to be carefully watched; insist that in the crisis of your country's history your first allegiance is to your country and not to any leader, executive, or committee, and you are forthwith a disturber, a factionist, a wrecker.

What is our programme? We at least, in conformity with the spirit of our movement, will try and tell it.

Our programme in time of peace was to gather into Irish hands in Irish trade unions the control of all the forces of production and distribution in Ireland. We never believed that freedom would be realised without fighting for it. From our earliest declaration of policy in Dublin in 1896 the editor of this paper has held to the dictum that our ends should be secured "peacefully if possible, forcibly if necessary." Believing so we saw what the world outside Ireland is realising to-day, that the destinies of the world and the fighting strength of armies are at the mercy of organised Labour as soon as that Labour becomes truly revolutionary. Thus we strove to make Labour in Ireland organised—and revolutionary.

We saw that should it come to a test in Ireland (as we hoped and prayed it might come), between those who stood for the Irish nation and those who stood for the foreign rule, the greatest civil asset in the hand of the Irish nation for use in the struggle would be the control of Irish docks, shipping, railways and production *(Continued on page 67)*

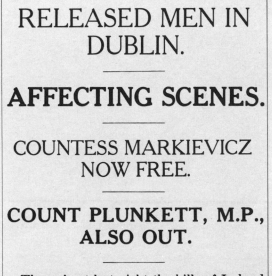

RELEASED MEN IN DUBLIN.

AFFECTING SCENES.

COUNTESS MARKIEVICZ NOW FREE.

COUNT PLUNKETT, M.P., ALSO OUT.

Throughout last night the hills of Ireland were ablaze with bonfires and the towns and villages were loud with the cheering of people and music of bands as Ireland greeted her returned prisoners. In the morning a group

(Left) Relatives visit Sinn Fein prisoners in the yard of Richmond Barracks, Dublin.

Crowds of Dubliners greet returning prisoners, June 18, 1917.

*Meanwhile Redmond, whose Parliamentary Party was burdened
by association with the growingly unpopular Home Rule
settlement, was rapidly losing ground among Irish voters to
Sinn Fein—pledged to complete independence.*

(Top) Michael Collins, coming to be important Sinn Fein leader, and (Bottom) Countess Markievicz campaigning for Sinn Fein candidates.

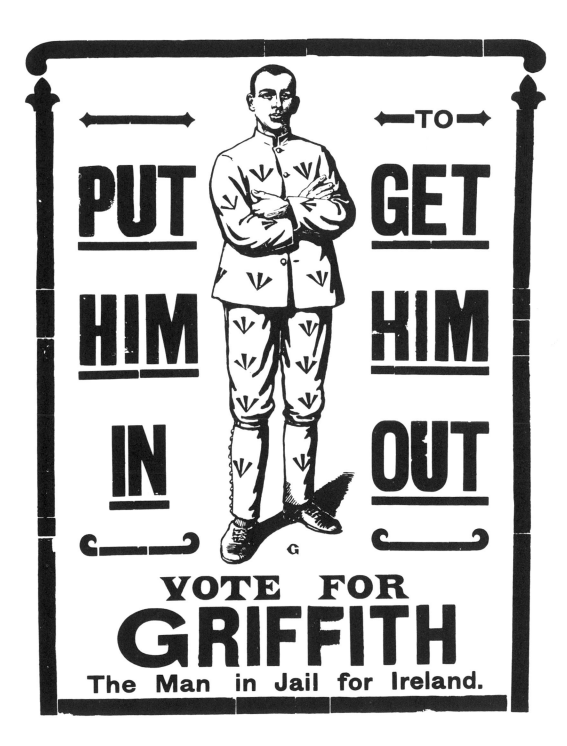

SOLDIERS ARE
E LIVES ARE PLEDGE

by Unions who gave sole allegiance to Ireland.

We realised that the power of the enemy to hurl his forces upon the forces of Ireland would lie at the mercy of the men who controlled the transport system of Ireland; we saw that the hopes of Ireland a Nation rested upon the due recognition of the identity of interest between that ideal and the rising hopes of Labour.

In Europe to-day we have seen the strongest governments of the world exerting every effort, holding out all possible sorts of inducement to Organised Labour to use its organisation on the side of those governments in time of war. We have spent the best part of our lifetime striving to create in Ireland the working class spirit that would create an Irish organisation of Labour willing to do voluntarily for Ireland what those governments of Europe are beseeching their trade unions to do for their countries. And we have partly succeeded.

We have succeeded in creating an organisation that will willingly do more for Ireland than any trade union in the world has attempted to do for its national government. Had we not been attacked and betrayed by many of our fervent advanced patriots, had they not been so anxious to destroy us, so willing to applaud even the British Government when it attacked us, had they stood by us and pushed our organisation all over Ireland it would now be in our power at a word to crumple up and demoralise every offensive move of the enemy against the champions of Irish freedom.

Had we been able to carry out all our plans, as such an Irish organisation of Labour alone could carry them out, we could at a word have created all the conditions necessary to the striking of a successful blow whenever the military arm of Ireland wished to move.

Have we a programme? We are the only people that had a programme—that understood the mechanical conditions of modern war, and the dependence of national power upon industrial control.

What is our programme now? At the grave risk of displeasing alike the perfervid Irish patriot and the British "competent military authority," we shall tell it.

We believe that in times of peace we should work along the lines of peace to strengthen the nation, and we believe that whatever strengthens and elevates the Working Class strengthens the nation.

But we also believe that in times of war we should act as in war. We despise, entirely despise and loathe, all the mouthings and mouthers about war who infest Ireland in time of peace, just as we despise and loathe all the cantings about caution and restraint to which the same people treat us in times of war.

Mark well then our programme. While the war lasts and Ireland still is a subject nation we shall continue to urge her to fight for her freedom.

We shall continue, in season and out of season, to teach that the "far-flung battle line" of England is weakest at the point nearest its heart, that Ireland is in that position of tactical advantage, that a defeat of England in India, Egypt, the Balkans or Flanders would not be so dangerous to the British Empire as any conflict of armed forces in Ireland, that the time for Ireland's Battle is NOW, the place for Ireland's Battle is HERE.

That a strong man may deal lusty blows with his fists against a host of surrounding foes and conquer, but will succumb if a child sticks a pin in his heart.

But the moment peace is once admitted by the British Government as *(Continued on page 78)*

Sinn Fein moved to constitute itself the official voice of the nation. A convention was called and a new constitution, demanding no less than an Irish Republic, adopted. De Valera was elected President, announced his intention of securing international recognition of independent Ireland . . .

De Valera and supporters celebrate election victory.

*. . . Only a year later, Sinn Fein was to sweep Ireland in the 1918
General Election, and its leaders shortly after were to convene
an independent "Constituent Assembly of the Irish Nation"—
known as Dail Eireann.*

First meeting of the Dail Eireann, January 21, 1919.

The Sinn Fein Leaders
L. to r.:—1st. row: L. Ginnell, M. Collins (leader of the Irish Republican Army), Cathal Brugha, Arthur Griffith (founder of the Sinn Fein), Eamon de Valera (President of the Irish Republic), Count Plunkett, E. MacNeill, William Cosgrave and E. Blythe.

2nd. row: P. Maloney, Terence McSwiney (Lord Mayor of Cork), Richard Mulcahy, J. O'Doherty, J. O'Mahony, J. Dolan, J. McGuinness, P. O'Keefe, Michael Staines, McGrath, Dr. B. Cussack, L. de Roiste, W. Colivet, Rev. Father Michael O'Flanagan (vice-president of the Sinn Fein).

3rd. row: P. War, A. McCabe, D. Fitzgerald, J. Sweeney, Dr. Hayes, C. Collins, P. O'Maillie, J. O'Mara, B. O'Higgins, J. Burke, and Kevin O'Higgins. 4th. row: J. McDonagh and J. McEntee. 5th. row: P. Beasely, R. Dartan and P. Galligan. 6th. row: P. Shanahan and S. Etchingham.

De Valera, president of the Irish Volunteers, reviews a section of his rapidly expanding army at Six-Mile Bridge, County Clare.

In April 1918 a new Man-Power Bill was presented in Commons,
calling for military conscription in Ireland. All Irish parties
were united in absolute opposition and drew up an
Anti-Conscription Pledge which was signed by virtually
the whole of nationalist Ireland.

"Denying the right of the British Government to enforce compulsory service in this country, we pledge ourselves solemnly
to one another to resist Conscription by the most effective means at our disposal."

*Resistance to conscription impressed the British with Ireland's
now-solidified national will: there was little ground left between
complete accession to Irish demands and simple use of force.
Field-Marshal Lord French (below), a believer in directly
military solutions, was named Lord-Lieutenant of Ireland.*

Lord French and General Macready (right), Commander in Chief of British forces in Ireland, reviewing British troops.

NO CONSC
STAND U

De Valera addressing anti-conscription rally at Ballahodreen.

*The arrest of one Joseph Dowling, sent by Germany to contact
Sinn Fein, provided the British with a pretext for arresting
leaders of Sinn Fein and the Volunteers—among them
Countess Markievicz, Arthur Griffith and de Valera—
and for returning many of them once more to English jails.*

being a subject ripe for discussion, *that moment our policy will be for peace* and in direct opposition to all talk or preparation for armed revolution.

We will be no party to leading out Irish patriots to meet the might of an England at peace. The moment peace is in the air we shall strictly confine ourselves, and lead all our influence to the work of turning the thought of Labour in Ireland to the work of peaceful reconstruction.

That is our programme. You can now compare it with the programme of those who bid you hold your hand now, and thus put it in the power of the enemy to patch up a temporary peace, turn round and smash you at his leisure, and then go to war again with the Irish question settled—in the graves of Irish patriots.

We fear that is what is going to happen. It is to our mind inconceivable that the British public should allow conscription to be applied to England and not to Ireland. Nor do the British Government desire it. But that Government will use the cry of the necessities of war to force conscription upon the people of England, and will then make a temporary peace, and turn round to force Ireland to accept the same terms as have been forced upon England.

The English public will gladly see this done—misfortune likes company. The situation will then

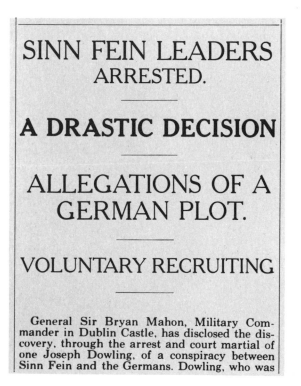

SINN FEIN LEADERS ARRESTED.

A DRASTIC DECISION

ALLEGATIONS OF A GERMAN PLOT.

VOLUNTARY RECRUITING

General Sir Bryan Mahon, Military Commander in Dublin Castle, has disclosed the discovery, through the arrest and court martial of one Joseph Dowling, of a conspiracy between Sinn Fein and the Germans. Dowling, who was

shape itself thus: The Irish Volunteers who are pledged to fight conscription will either need to swallow their pledge, and see the young men of Ireland conscripted, or will need to resent conscription, and engage the military force of England at a time when England is at peace.

This is what the diplomacy of England is working for, what the stupidity of some of our leaders who imagine they are Wolfe Tones is making possible. It is our duty, it is the duty of all who wish to save Ireland from such shame or such slaughter to strengthen the hand of those of the leaders who are for action as against those who are playing into the hands of the enemy.

We are neither rash nor cowardly. We know our opportunity when we see it, and we know when it has gone. We know that at the end of this war England will have at least an army of one million men, or *more than two soldiers for every adult male in Ireland*. And these soldiers will be veterans of the greatest war in history.

We shall not want to fight those men. We shall devote our attention to organising their comrades who return to civil life, to organising them into trade unions and into Labour parties to secure them their right in civil life.

Unless we emigrate to some country where there are men.□

*The Armistice of November 11, 1918, which created
scenes of rejoicing—like that below in London—
through most of the Western world . . .*

. . . found in Ireland only the continuation of struggle between a British government now committed to partition and an Irish people ever determined to have an integral and completely independent country.

After a skirmish between Sinn Feiners and the R.I.C. on the outskirts of Tralee: one R.I.C. cadet wounded (foreground), and three Sinn Feiners dead.

Members of Sinn Fein being taken to jail.

"...We Ourselves..."

IN my youth—that is, more or less around the turn of the 20th century—Ireland was already in the throes of what was to prove her ultimate national revival. Three things provided this revival with its essential sources of energy and public feeling: Ireland's memories of the dead and martyred heroes of the centuries-old, if intermittent, struggle for independence; the renaissance of Ireland's language and cultural tradition; and a growing despair over the so recently promised possibility that England at last would grant Ireland some measure of Home Rule. The heroic memories still had something of a present embodiment in the Irish Republican Brotherhood, the secret Fenian society whose tiny but dedicated membership could claim direct descent from the revolutionaries of 1848, from James Stephens and his associates who had languished after 1865 in English jails, and from Jeremiah O'Donovan Rossa. Small and secret though it was, and ridden with police spies, the I.R.B. had its sources of strength, among them the backing of the *Clan na Gael* in the United States. Its leaders were preparing to constitute themselves a Provisional Government in the event of a revolution. The cultural renaissance, which, though it was a movement without any direct political content, perhaps more than anything else laid the ground for the national feeling that was to have such enormous political consequences in the years 1916-1922, was expressed most centrally through the Gaelic League. The Gaelic League had been founded in 1893 by Dr. Douglas Hyde; the new consciousness that it fostered was officially translated into the will for national self-determination through the organization of Sinn Fein by Arthur Griffith in 1905. Indeed, it may be said that these twin movements—the Gaelic League and Sinn Fein —*were* the Irish national revival. In any case, I myself came very early to participate actively in all three groups and could thus, I suppose, have been called the complete Irish nationalist.

It was not until 1914, however, that most of us were forced to give up the hope that Ireland might yet achieve the kind of independence she needed and longed for within the British Empire. The Irish Parliamentary party in the British House of Commons, the party of the fallen Parnell and, now, of John Redmond, had for at least four years before then been bringing the word to Ireland that the long Parliamentary battle for Irish Home Rule, for an Irish Parliament legislating for Irishmen in Dublin, was soon to be crowned with success. In 1910 the Liberal party had, in the election that was called "the Great Home Rule Election," been given a clear mandate, and in 1911 the Parliament Act had so restricted the power of the Lords— enemies of Home Rule—to veto bills passed in Commons, that Redmond and his party believed they would see an Irish Parliament in Dublin before the end of 1913. There were, to be sure, men all over Ireland, and particularly in the I.R.B., for whom mere Home Rule without a full and final separation from England could never have answered to their dream of national independence. Nevertheless, even so incomplete an autonomy as would have been purchased by an Irish Parliament was felt among the people and many of the leaders of Sinn Fein to be a great advance in Irish fortunes. But as 1914 wore on, it became clear that the British government was capitulating to the opposition within Ireland and England. Home Rule was to be a truncated affair, Ireland herself might very well suffer truncation—through the physical partition of those counties loyal to Ireland and those loyal to England—and even so small and sad a freedom could not be attained until after the great war that was about to engulf Europe.

As it happened—and it was not the least of many

by Sean T. O'Kelly

*As incidence of violence between Irish insurgents and British
troops continues to mount, De Valera escapes from Lincoln
Gaol and sets out for America. His mission: to float a loan for the
Dail and secure recognition by the United States
government for the Republic of Ireland.*

ironies that had helped to shape Irish history—the "absolute" nationalists among us were being abetted by those in Belfast, and in the six northern counties collectively called "Ulster," who were staunch Unionists—that is, members of the party which demanded that Ireland remain completely under English hegemony. For the Ulster Unionists, by their intransigence in Westminster (in which they were supported by the Conservatives) and by their having raised a citizen army which threatened rebellion at the institution of Home Rule, succeeded in undermining its implementation to the point where only sterner measures would serve to further the cause of Irish independence.

The I.R.B., for which I had been serving as a voluntary organizer since 1902, watched developments in Ulster with great interest. Whatever the concern for the power of the Unionists to disrupt the implementation of Home Rule, there were those among us who could not fail to take heart from the spectacle of Irishmen openly preaching insurrection against the Crown and arming themselves for acts of rebellion. "They are doing our work," it was whispered in the inner councils of the I.R.B.; if the Orangemen are arming illegally with the connivance of the pro-Union authorities and the Conservative party, well then they are setting a priceless precedent for others,

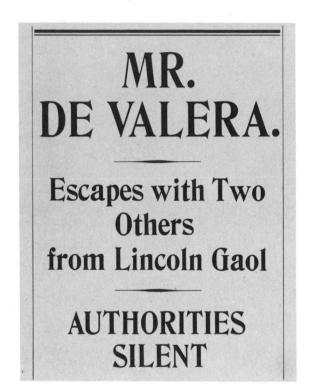

MR. DE VALERA.

Escapes with Two Others from Lincoln Gaol

AUTHORITIES SILENT

with other ends in view, to arm as well. And indeed, on November 25, 1913, at a memorable meeting in Dublin's Rotunda Rink, Eoin MacNeill called together thousands of his fellow citizens to enroll in a new military organization called the Irish Volunteers. So successful was MacNeill's appeal that the Rotunda Rink could not accommodate the huge crowds of people who showed up for the meeting; I had to take charge of an overflow meeting for which we quickly had to hire a neighboring hall. Meetings of this kind subsequently took place in practically every parish in Ireland: in six months' time the Irish Volunteers had recruited nearly one hundred thousand men.

The new organization of Volunteers was all too soon to suffer tribulations. Called together, as its constitution declared, "To Defend the Rights and Liberties of all Irishmen," Britain's declaration of war on Germany confronted it with certain naked choices about where the best service to those rights and liberties lay. Redmond on behalf of the Parliamentary party, committed to dealing in Westminster for Ireland's future, naturally demanded the right to control the Volunteers for his purposes. The Executive of the Volunteers split into two groups over this demand. On the one hand, Redmond had great power and a great *(Continued on page 93)*

(Right) De Valera at a rally in Boston.

Dubliners retreat before a baton charge of the R.I.C.

After an ambush in Capel St., Dublin.

*Addressing the Dail, de Valera had declared the Irish Republic
the only lawful authority in Ireland. Thus British forces were
now to be regarded as an invading army with whom the
Irish were openly and irrevocably at war.*

Black and Tans search suspected Sinn Feiner.

*The Volunteers—soon to become officially the Irish Republican
Army—were being organized by Cathal Brugha and
Michael Collins to conduct guerrilla warfare. Meanwhile,
French's army helped police to break up meetings,
smash presses, and carry out raids into homes and offices.*

(Top) Members of Sinn Fein club in Manchester before the court on charges of manslaughter after attack on police raiders
which wounded two policemen.
(Bottom) IRA internees in Dublin, 1920, cover their faces to avoid photographer.

A famous IRA unit, the Mayo Flying Column, who in a battle at Tourmakeady were reputed to have held off six hundred British troops.

*Raids, arrests, and shootings intensified. In a special enactment
called "the Restoration of Order in Ireland Act," Parliament
empowered military authorities to make blanket searches and
seizures and arrests of anyone swearing allegiance to the Dail.*

following among the recruits. On the other hand, men like Griffith and some of the leaders of the I.R.B. were absolutely immovable on one point: Ireland must not be partitioned—the solution now promised in Parliamentary negotiation. As Griffith stated in an editorial in his paper, *Sinn Fein,* on July 11th, 1914: "We would give much to see a national legislature, no matter how limited its scope, reestablished in this country, for, poor though the thing might be, it would give us again a national center. But this 'Home Rule' no longer proposes to set up such a legislature—instead it proposes to cut Ireland in two and to stereotype the vanishing differences between Southern and Northern, Catholic and Protestant. We tell those who would accept such a measure and think it gain that they will bring not peace to Ireland, but a poisoned sword." When Redmond announced his support for Britain against Germany and appealed to Irishmen to join the British army, the Volunteers itself was split apart. Redmond marched off with his followers, leaving behind an organization of only twenty thousand—depleted in ranks but distilled and clarified in purpose.

With England now at war it was inevitable that the leaders of the Volunteers and those of us who were their friends and associates should begin to do some hard thinking about how to take advan-

TONIGHT AT TWELVE O'CLOCK

Dublin Passes Under Control of the Military

ADVICE TO CITIZENS.

PROCLAMATION IN FORCE AS OF MIDNIGHT

tage of the period ahead for Ireland. For years the motto of those who cherished the dream of complete freedom had been, "England's difficulty is Ireland's opportunity." And after all, we had at our disposal an organization of twenty thousand men, a good number of whom were armed. Thus it was that one day Tom Clarke, a revolutionary who had returned among us after long years of imprisonment and who was both a friend and a source of inspiration to me, informed me that he meant to call a meeting of a few passionately interested people to discuss what we might do. This was in September 1914. I suggested that we meet at 25 Parnell Square, headquarters of the Gaelic League, because this place was not under police surveillance. The meeting took place some few days later. Present were Tom Clarke, Sean MacDermott, Padraic Pearse, Thomas McDonagh, Arthur Griffith, Major Sean McBride, Eamon Ceannt, Joseph Mary Plunkett, James Connolly, William O'Brien, Sean Tobin, Sean McGarry and myself. We decided, first, that we must do everything possible to strengthen the Volunteers and the Citizen Army—the radical group headed by James Connolly—and to get new recruits for these groups as well as for the *Fianna,* the scout organization led by Countess Markievicz, and the women's orga- *(Continued on page 98)*

(Left) British soldiers prepare gun emplacement outside Mountjoy Prison in Dublin.

British soldiers on the roof of the Four Courts, guarding the Liffey embankment—1920.

*Republican prisoners in British jails had consistently demanded,
and been denied, treatment as prisoners of war. In Mountjoy
prison in Dublin, and in Wormwood Scrubs prison in London,
Sinn Fein prisoners resorted to a hunger-strike. . .*

nization, the *Cumann na mBan*. Second, we must be prepared to resist any attempt by the British to enforce conscription in Ireland or to disarm the Volunteers. Third, if a German force were to land in Ireland and were to promise us help in gaining independence, we would offer them our cooperation. And finally we agreed that before the war's end we should proclaim the independence of Ireland and make an armed insurrection: this would give us the right to claim a seat at the peace conference to be held after the war as belligerents.

In March of 1915 I was sent on a secret mission to the United States to contact the *Clan na Gael* and inform them of the plans for an insurrection in Ireland. I was to contact John Devoy, Judge Cohalan, and Joseph McGarrity and ask them for whatever money the *Clan na Gael* could give us. I was told only what I had to know, and no date for the insurrection was mentioned. In order to avoid the police, I mapped for myself a devious course to America. I boarded a tram for Dalkey, and there took the train for Greystones, where my younger brother Michael met me with my small suitcase. Then I headed for Rosslare and boarded a boat for Farnborough, England. After a two days' visit with my married sister in Farnborough, I traveled to Liverpool, took a third-class berth on the s/s St. Paul, and

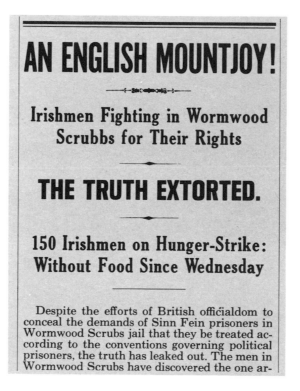

AN ENGLISH MOUNTJOY!

Irishmen Fighting in Wormwood Scrubbs for Their Rights

THE TRUTH EXTORTED.

150 Irishmen on Hunger-Strike: Without Food Since Wednesday

Despite the efforts of British officialdom to conceal the demands of Sinn Fein prisoners in Wormwood Scrubs jail that they be treated according to the conventions governing political prisoners, the truth has leaked out. The men in Wormwood Scrubs have discovered the one ar-

set off on an extremely uncomfortable sailing to New York.

One way and another I got in touch with my three contacts, one of whom, Joseph McGarrity, lived in Philadelphia. It took nearly a month for them to get together the money I was to take back with me. The morning I was due to sail home I met with Denis Spellissey, who was an officer of the *Clan*. Spellissey arrived with two large and heavy cardboard boxes which, he told me, contained the money. Each of the boxes held one thousand English sovereigns: he had thought it would make a glorious gesture for us to buy the arms with which we were to fight the English with English gold, and he had gone to enormous trouble to get hold of sovereigns. I suggested, as gently as I could considering my hurry, that the gesture be preserved in memory — his and mine — and that he hurry to a bank and exchange the gold for twenty-five- and fifty-pound notes. He was, as I could see, disappointed, but I shuddered to imagine myself trying to get through customs and the long journey ahead with two large cardboard boxes filled with gold. Back in Dublin, I gave Tom Clarke one thousand pounds for the I.R.B. and Eoin MacNeill one thousand pounds for the Volunteers.

I knew nothing, as I *(Continued on page 107)*

. . . while crowds of sympathizers gathered outside both prisons, praying and chanting Fenian songs. In London, a group of praying men and women were attacked by an angry mob as police stood by. Eventually hunger strikers were released.

Women dressed in mourning say their rosaries for Republican prisoners sentenced to execution.

(Above) Sentries examining parcels being brought to Republican prisoners in Mountjoy.

(Right) British troops, tanks, and armored cars guarding the entrance to Mountjoy.

[100]

*Meanwhile, Irish guerrilla activity was steadily increasing.
In June and July of 1920 there were more than fifty I.R.A. raids
on British emplacements and government buildings—producing
in turn a stepped-up round of British reprisals.*

British examine wreckage of sabotaged train.

By 1921, in addition to the sacking of Republican homes and
villages and wholesale summary arrests, the British were once
more to reply to Irish insurgence with the pistol and firing squad
—at an estimated average of one shooting a day.

Members of Cumann na mBan, Irishwomen's Council, wave encouragement to Mountjoy prisoners over top of wall.

Crowd protesting the execution of six prisoners in Dublin.

CORK LORD MAYOR
ARRESTED

THE THIRTIETH
"In Life or Death the Victory is
Says Lord Mayor of Cork.

SPIRITED AWAY"
rd Mayor of Cork Tak
Off in Destroyer

BOY PRISONER'S STRUG

ONE PENNY.

THE FREEMAN'S

"AT DEATH'S DO
rd Mayor and Conditi
Mountjoy Prisoners

REMOVED TO THE
COUNTY JAIL

hat is the Charge Against
Cork Lord Mayor?

Rule from Ballast town.

A SILENT VIGIL
By the Bedside of the
Dying Lord Mayor

LORD MAYOR
OF CORK

ateful Reply to Findi
of Courtmartial

NOT TAKING FOO

IN THE NAME OF HUMANITY.
The Lord Mayor of Dublin has issued the following
through the Freeman's Journal:—

"AN APPEAL TO THE PEOPLE of
GREAT BRITAIN

have said, about the intended date for the uprising. But in the months that followed, our activities were going constantly forward and our orders seemed to be getting more and more urgent. During this time, several prominent members of the movement were arrested and given the choice of going into exile in England or going to jail. One day Padraic Pearse asked me to get him maps of the Dublin sewers and also outlines of the city's major electrical circuits. It was clear that military plans of some kind were being made. Pearse asked me to serve on his staff; when the operations started, he told me, he was to be in command.

In the month before Easter many meetings were held, and then just before Easter I had a letter from Pearse asking me if he and his brother might stay at my house over the Easter week-end. Important maneuvers had been fixed for Easter, and he wanted to stay with us as our house was nearer to Liberty Hall than his own. On that Saturday night, all was confusion. There was bad news about the blowing up of a shipment of arms and ammunition sent from Germany in Cork Harbor. Roger Casement, just arrived himself from Germany, had been apprehended on the coast of Kerry and taken into custody by the British. MacNeill, who had ordered the Easter maneuvers, was upset—by the bad news as well as by the realization that his maneuvers were to be used as the springboard for an insurrection he was certain was doomed to failure. (He did, in fact, the next day issue a public notice calling off the maneuvers, but by then it was too late to stem the tide.)

THE RISING

Thinking back on Easter Monday 1916, my most vivid memories — undoubtedly as do those of any individual who participates in a large event — present themselves to me in a fragmentary and entirely personal way. Finally the things that come to one most clearly are the things that happened in one's own corner of the event, that happened to oneself. Well, then, on Monday morning I was out of the house early, stopped at my office, stopped to see my mother, and about 11 o'clock made my way to Liberty Hall. A crowd was there, milling around in considerable confusion. I saw Pearse. He asked if I was with him, and I said yes. Then someone — it must, I think, have been James Connolly—said to form up, and a small column of us marched to the General Post Office in O'Connell Street. And the Easter Rebellion of 1916 was under way.

Once inside the Post Office we were, at first, a little bewildered. Then someone who knew the building showed Tom Clarke, Sean MacDermott, and Padraic Pearse into a large room upstairs.

*With McSwiney and fellow-prisoners from Cork calling the
attention of the world to Ireland by their lengthening
hunger-strike, the realization grows in England that the Irish
problem is now utterly beyond any convenient settlement . . .*

They talked quietly for a while, and Pearse went downstairs to join Connolly, who was in the meantime busily giving orders. He asked to have the building cleared of all the Post Office officials, then he ordered some of the men to knock all the windows out of the building and have them sandbagged. Meanwhile I had been standing around, waiting to be of service to Pearse, wondering what I was to do. Connolly saw me and told me to go to Liberty Hall. In a certain room on a certain press I would find a large parcel wrapped in brown paper; in the parcel were two flags, one a green-orange-and-white Tricolor and the other an all-green flag with a gold harp in the center. I was to bring him these two flags. I did as Connolly told me, and when I handed him the flags he called over someone standing by and ordered him to hoist the flags on two flagpoles on the roof of the G.P.O. building. And with this, Commandant-General Connolly had become Commander of the Republican forces in Dublin.

Some time after we had occupied the G.P.O. we received word that a company of British cavalry was advancing on O'Connell Street. Thirty or forty men were sent out to form a line across the street and intercept the British. In a few minutes we saw a column of Lancers galloping into O'Connell Street, the crowd that had been milling about in front of the Post Office scattered and took cover in the side streets, several shots rang out, and then we could see the Lancers retreating in confusion, in all directions, having left a few of their men and some of their horses behind lying on the pavement.

My next mission was to return once more to Liberty Hall, see that it was evacuated and that all the munitions which had been collected there were brought to Connolly in the G.P.O. When I reached Liberty Hall, I found Captain McGowan, to whom I was to relay the orders, and about five or six of his friends in one room. They were sitting on boxes — a few were on the floor — manufacturing bombs. Powder and shot and bits of scrap iron were arranged in piles on the floor between the men. In one corner there was a separate small heap of percussion caps and scraps of copper wire, and right in the middle of the floor was a pile of assorted tin cans and canisters. Each of these tin cans was handed from one man to the next, assembly-line style, and each man deposited in it a certain quota of the material on the floor in front of him. The last man fixed the wire and percussion cap and put on the lid.

When I was able to inform General Connolly that both munitions and munitions makers had been deployed as he requested, I was told to take a

(Above) A severe shortage of coal drives Dublin citizenry into raiding coal yard for daily supplies.

dozen men and go out and commandeer a large stock of bread and milk. We covered shops and dairies in the neighborhood until we had filled all the handcarts we had taken with us. Commandeering proved to be a somewhat discomfiting task for me; though I understood the need for it, and that we were, in effect, in a state of war, some part of me shared in the shopkeepers' and dairy-keepers' view of what I was doing: in short, that I was leading a band of thieves and looters. I scrupulously gave them all receipts for what I was taking, and announced to them that one day the Government of the Irish Republic would honor these receipts — a gesture that seemed to go only a very short way toward reassuring them.

Later in the day, some three or four hundred people gathered in front of the G.P.O. to hear Commandant - General Pearse read aloud the Proclamation of the Republic. When the reading, and the determined cheering that attended it, was finished, Connolly called my name. "Captain O'Kelly, what are you doing?" "Nothing, sir," in my newly-assumed military manner. "Well," he ordered, "take these copies of the Proclamation and have them pasted up around the city." I had no paste, so I collected a few idle men and after some consultation, I led my second commandeering expedition: we broke into various shops, got the necessary flour, buckets, brushes, etc., returned to the G.P.O., went into the basement, and made the paste. Then we posted about two hundred Proclamations through the streets of Dublin. And thus can it be said that I had my part in making known the Republic.

During the afternoon Connolly heard that the British were moving in from the direction of Dollymount and that they were being engaged by a group of Volunteers at Clontarf. I was told to take thirty riflemen to Clontarf as reinforcements. I found thirty volunteers for the job in no time, but was then faced with the problem — quite beyond my experience — of how to get them into proper formation. Fortunately for me one of the thirty men, Thomas Craven, had been a captain in the Liverpool Volunteers. Captain Craven lined up the men, barked the required orders, and off we marched in the direction of Clontarf. We set up our H.Q. in the offices of the manure works at Fairview and sent out some scouts to locate the British. The report had been unfounded; we found no British, and returned to the Post Office, Captain Craven and I marching at the head of our company.

My next orders were to take some men, go to the other side of O'Connell Street, and disperse a gang of looters who were raiding the shops there.

(Above) Crowd of Dubliners makes an attempt on a British barricade.

This assignment was for me an impossible one. Each time we managed to clear the mob out of one shop—threatening, pushing, chasing, shooting our guns—they would simply move on to another. I returned across the street and explained the situation to Connolly. He asked if I had shot anyone. I said no, but that we had fired shots over the heads of the mob. "Shooting over their heads is useless," he told me. "Unless a few of them are shot you won't be able to stop them." The General granted my request to be released from this duty.

By now it must have been seven o'clock, and I had as yet had nothing to eat. I went upstairs in the G.P.O. and took tea with my friends, the signers of the Proclamation, in their quarters. Joseph Plunkett was there. Plunkett had undergone an operation a couple of weeks earlier, and was still quite ill; he was lying on a mattress on the floor, determined not to miss being part of the great event. Everyone demanded to hear an account of my day, and, I am afraid, there was a good deal of merriment at my expense.

About 10 o'clock Sean MacDermott came to me with a delicate assignment. Bulmer Hobson, who had been arrested on Good Friday by his fellow members of the Supreme Council of the I.R.B. for, presumably, opposing the plans for the Easter Rising, was incarcerated in a private house in

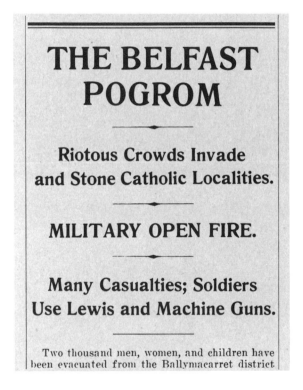

THE BELFAST POGROM

Riotous Crowds Invade and Stone Catholic Localities.

MILITARY OPEN FIRE.

Many Casualties; Soldiers Use Lewis and Machine Guns.

Two thousand men, women, and children have been evacuated from the Ballymacarret district.

Cabra Park. They had now decided to release him, and I was to go and inform him of this. I went off and made my way through the deserted streets of North Dublin. There was nothing to be seen, but I could hear shots coming from all quarters of the city—a steady tattoo of single gun-shots, as if snipers were firing at one another from the roof-tops. Hobson and those who were holding him were naturally relieved when they heard my orders. We all walked down the street together while I told them whatever I could about the day's happenings.

Before I had left for Cabra Park, Tom Clarke asked me, since I was going to the North side of the city, please to deliver a letter to his wife at their home in Richmond Park. Mrs. Clarke received her letter calmly and resolutely. We talked a while; she asked me if I had any word of her brother, Ned Daly, who was in command of the First Battalion of the Volunteers at Four Courts. I returned by way of my own mother's house, and consoled her a little for her absent children.

Then for the last time on that long and crowded day I returned to the Post Office. It was 2 A.M., and finally I found a spot under the front counter of the main hall of the Post Office, collected some mail bags for pillow and mattress, borrowed some blankets, and crawled under them for a bit of sleep. □

(Right) Catholic shipyard workers being pursued along York Street in Belfast during anti-Catholic riot.

Scene of an election celebration in Belfast during which Unionists painted walls throughout the city in red, white, and blue.

Sir James Craig, Unionist leader, addressing Protestant workers in Belfast shipyard: "Do I approve of the action you boys have taken . . . ? I say yes."

British soldiers frisk an Irish citizen for weapons.

A Terrible Beauty

In the very far west of the County Donegal, which is the northwestern humped-up shoulder of Ireland, there is a little village called Frosses. It is noticeable chiefly because the world we live in is on one side of the street and the next world on the other side. On one side, that is, are houses and shops, and on the other, the church and the churchyard, and in the churchyard is the chief possession of the village: the grave of a woman who was a poet.

When she wrote her poems she called herself Ethna Carbery. She died young in the year 1902. She was not a very notable poet but the slight book of verse and songs and ballads, *The Four Winds of Erin,* by which she deserves to be remembered is interesting in that it mirrors pretty well something of what was in the minds of the young Irish people of her time, the young people influenced by the work of Douglas Hyde and the Gaelic League, by pride in the rediscovered possession of a native language, and in a past in which even the recurring failure of rebellion against the rule of imperial London became a matter for renewed passion and high romance. They had youth and hope and that fearless desire for conflict that in 1966 seems so naive, as innocent as something in the ancient heroic tales. Their minds were indeed fed on those ancient heroic tales. In her little title poem about the four winds of Erin, Ethna Carbery had one of those statuesque female figures used by the poets to symbolize Ireland, one of those young women with the walk of a queen, stating her preference for "the black, black wind from the Northern hills," because that Northern wind had "rustled oft through Aileach's halls and stirred the hair of Hugh." That Hugh was the great O'Neill, the Earl of Tyrone, who fought to the end and death in exile against the first Elizabeth. According to legend he and his followers sat in faery trance under the hill of Aileach waiting for the day to come when they would awake again to take part in the liberating of Ireland. AE and William Yeats were talking to each other about the return of the ancient Celtic gods to the seven sacred mountains of Ireland. It was part of the messianic, apocalyptic mood of the time that the gods should return to dwell on the hills and the heroes dream under the hills until the day should dawn and the hour strike.

But that young poetess also wrote a ballad, still much sung, about Rody McCorley, an Ulster rebel of 1798 who was hanged at Toomebridge on the shores of Lough Neagh. Behind her ballad there is an older one, which I collected from an old man in Toomebridge, that tells in detail the story of the life and death of Rody, one of those "boys of the heather" who never quite make the history books but who live clearly in the folk memory. The old ballad begins: *"Come tender-hearted Christians, all attention to me pay/Till I relate these verses great, these verses two or three,/Concerning of a noble youth who was cut off in his bloom/And died upon the gallows tree near to the Bridge of Toome."*

Her later song recounts: *"Up the narrow street he stepped/Smiling, proud and young./About the hemp rope on his neck/The golden ringlets clung."* The hempen cravat, the walk to the gallows, was the expected fate of the young hero, expected even by himself, who had dreamed his way into the silences under the hills and been possessed by the spirits of the great ones of the past. Yeats was to write: *"When Pearse summoned Cuchulain to his side,/What stalked through the Post Office?"*

Ethna Carbery's friend, the poet and playwright, Alice Milligan (1866-1953), is most remembered for catching in one simple poem a memory of the time when she was a little girl in a garden playing.

by Benedict Kiely

British troops sweep through an Irish village on a search for Sinn Feiners and arms.

During twelve months of 1920 the number of unarmed persons
killed by Crown Forces was 203. British Labor Commission, in
preparing a special report, cited not only destruction of life
but "wanton destruction of economic Ireland."

The ogres that her old nurse in the Church of Ireland rectory in Omagh, County Tyrone, used to invoke to frighten the children into obedience were the Fenians, the rebels of 1867, who in the old nurse's stories were an army of papists grim with a green flag o'er them, and red coats and black police flying before them. But God, who, according to the old nurse, guarded British dominions and who had sent the storm that ended the Armada had sent also in the terrible weather of 1867 a great fall of snow and scattered the Fenians. In the rectory nursery the children listened in fright to the nurse's tales, but little Alice, predestined to take her part with the people of Ireland, watched the others with laughter and thought that when the Fenians came she would rise and go after: *"Wished she had been a boy/And a good deal older—/Able to walk for miles/With a gun on her shoulder."*

The memory of the Fenians on the hills in that bitter snow, of an abortive rebellion that had provoked more passion and song, sad and defiant, than any event since that calamitous "first year of liberty," 1798, was smouldering, ready for reawakening in the Irish heart. Pearse blew it into flame in 1915 in a remarkable piece of oratory, that was a sort of declaration of war, at a graveside in Glasnevin when that "unrepentant Fenian," Jeremiah

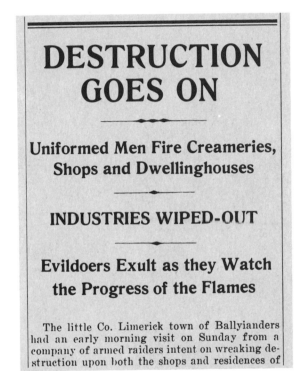

DESTRUCTION GOES ON

Uniformed Men Fire Creameries, Shops and Dwellinghouses

INDUSTRIES WIPED-OUT

Evildoers Exult as they Watch the Progress of the Flames

The little Co. Limerick town of Ballyianders had an early morning visit on Sunday from a company of armed raiders intent on wreaking destruction upon both the shops and residences of

O'Donovan Rossa, came back in his coffin from the life of imprisonment and then exile in the States that London rule had forced on him. Pearse cried out in defiance of that London government: "But the fools, the fools, the fools, they have left us our Fenian dead and while Ireland holds these graves Ireland unfree shall never be at peace."

Not only the Fenians dead but the Fenians alive were still having an influence on the people.

Tom Clarke, the Fenian, released from prison, kept his shop in Parnell Street in Dublin City and—a little distance away from the oddly-shaped monument to the leader dragged down by the most unholy alliance of the nonconformist conscience, the Irish party and the *"hysterica passio"* of a faction of the Irish—was an influence on the younger men and was to go to his death as one of the signatories of the 1916 Proclamation of the Irish Republic. John O'Leary, the Fenian, also returned from prison and exile and, very much alive, was to set standards in dignity and intellect for younger men. He had, as a young poet called Yeats was to observe and afterwards write down, personality, "a point of view not made for the crowd's sake but for self-expression." This made him magnetic to the generation to which Yeats belonged, and O'Leary had grown up: ". . . in a European move- *(Continued on page 129)*

(Left) A detachment of Gordon Highlanders guarding cars containing military stores.

The village of Knockcroghery after a British raid in which six houses were fired.

Vengeance for the death of a British soldier wreaked on the town of Balbriggan.

*Famous incident in Talbot Street: Sean Treacy, Vice-Commandant
of Tipperary No. 3 Brigade, in a gun duel with two British
intelligence officers, kills one officer and fatally wounds another, is
then himself fatally shot by a third agent . . .*

1

2

5

6

*. . . In the melee several bystanders are hit by bullets. The
dead are removed to British lorries and taken away.*

3

4

7

8

BLANKETS
PRESCOTTS'
DYE WORKS
TALBOT STREET DUBLIN

EVENING HERALD

6.30

£1 TO £1
KELLY'S GREAT
48 FLEET STR

VOL. 29.   No. 254.   DUBLIN, MONDAY, OCTOBER 25, 1920.   PRICE THREE HALFPENCE.

The Supreme Sacrifice—Lord Mayor's Death in Brixt

THE CURTAIN FALLS

Tragic Ending of Terrible Drama in Brixton

LORD MAYOR OF CORK'S DEATH

The terrible drama being enacted in Brixton Prison came to an end this morning when Alderman Terence MacSwiney, Lord Mayor of Cork, died on the seventy-fourth day of his hunger-strike.

Thus for the second time within twelve months the Rebel City has been deprived of its chief magistrate under circumstances which will cause a thrill of horror throughout the civilised world.

His predecessor in office Ald. T. MacCurtain, was, it will be remembered, done to death on the morning of March 19, and at the subsequent inquest a verdict of wilful murder was returned against David Lloyd George, Prime Minister of England; Lord French, Lord Lieutenant of Ireland; Ins. Macpherson, late Chief Secretary for Ireland; Acting-Inspector General Smith, of the R.I.C.; Divisional Inspector Clayton, of the R.I.C.; D.I. Swanzy, and some unknown members of the R.I.C.

THE LAST MOMENTS

[column of text, partially legible]

THE FINAL SCENE

[column of text]

COUNTRY'S GRIEF

Messages of Sympathy at Northern Councils

When the Lord Mayor of Dublin heard of the sad news he sent the following message to Mrs. MacSwiney:—

"Deepest sympathy to you in your terrible affliction."

A special meeting of the Corporation has been summoned for Wednesday at 1 p.m. to express regret of the city, and to tender sympathy to the family and the people of Cork.

AT NEWRY

[column of text]

CITY HEMMED IN

Military Stationed at All Exits

HOLDS UP AND SEARCHES

[column of text]

AT THE PORT

[column of text]

STOPPED AND SEARCHED

[column of text]

SISTER'S ORDEAL

[column of text]

SIMULTANEOUS

Mails Seized by Raiders in Co. Donegal

[column of text]

ACCIDENT IN THE CITY.

Carriage Overturned in Beresford Place.

[column of text]

THE NEWS IN CORK

Determined Statement by Deputy Lord Mayor

[column of text]

STATEMENT TO PRESS.

[column of text]

THE LATE ALDERMAN MacSWINEY

A USEFUL CAREER

Brief Sketch of the Patriot's Life

[column of text]

AN ARDENT STUDENT.

[column of text]

HIS LITERARY BENT.

[column of text]

INTO THE MOVEMENT

[column of text]

THE LADY MAYORESS

[column of text]

ARREST FOLLOWS ARREST.

[column of text]

NATION'S TRIBUTE.

The following is a copy of a telegram sent this morning by Mr. Arthur Griffith to the Lady Mayoress of Cork, Brixton, England:—

"Ireland mourns with you on the death of your hero husband. The nation for which the Lord Mayor of Cork died enshrines his memory for ever in its heart. He has proved what he said—that victory in this struggle for Ireland's freedom is not to those who can inflict most, but to those who can endure. The might of his country's enemies failed to check his faith or break his will. In death he exemplifies to mankind the truth that the spirit of the Irish nation is indestructible and unconquerable."

(Signed) ARTHUR GRIFFITH.

THE WIDOW AND ORPHAN.

COAL HOPES

Premier Meets Miners' Leaders To-day

BRIGHTER OUTLOOK

[column of text]

OTHER INDUSTRIES HIT.

[column of text]

IMPROVED PROSPECTS.

[column of text]

AT 10 DOWNING STREET.

[column of text]

A BAD TURN.

[column of text]

BELFAST RIOTS

Inquests on Three More Victims

[column of text]

DOCTORS ON THE SCENE.

[column of text]

HEATED ILL-FEELING.

[column of text]

MARTYR MAYOR

Patriot Prisoner's Peac Exit

DEATH-BED SCENE

We publish hereunder a graphic account by the special representative of the "Evening Herald" in London of the final moments of Brixton Prison of Ireland's latest martyr.

The material is supplied by the Rev. Fr. Dominic, O.S.F.C.

Lord Mayor's chaplain, and it constitute a poignant heroic self-sacrifice and unflinching determination.

A GRAPHIC ACCOUNT

[column of text]

THE END.

[column of text]

£1 TO £1
KELLY'S GREAT
48 FLEET STR

OUTSTANDING D

The following are outstanding dates in the Alderman Mr. MacSwiney over the past year:—
Elected Lord Mayor
Arrested
Started on hunger-strike
Tried by court martial
Deported
Died

REQUESTED PASS.

[column of text]

AN INQUEST.

[column of text]

ITEMS OF THE TRAGEDY.

[column of text]

*MacSwiney's death and funeral (below), an occasion for deep
mourning in Ireland, set off a wave of revulsion and shame in
London, where citizens stood in silence as coffin was
carried through the streets.*

ment when the revolutionist thought that he, above all men, must appeal to the highest motive, be guided by some ideal principle, be a little like Cato or Brutus, and he had lived to see the change Dostoevsky examined in *The Possessed.*"

Tom Clarke and John O'Leary in Dublin were the greatest survivors of a notable breed. There were others here and there all over the country. In one of his early stories of revolution Daniel Corkery wrote about one such old man in a Munster village: "I saw that every extreme movement in Ireland leaves behind it a remnant of its broken army, an old workman in a factory in a city, a cobbler in a little shop in a village, or . . . a shepherd in a hut on a mountainside—great old hearts that preserve to the next generation, even to the second next, the spark of fire that they themselves had received in the self-same manner from those that long since were gone home into the silence. Old embers that seem extinct and grey, Oisins dreaming of the heroic dead they have so long outlived, ineffectual in a thousand cases, except to raise jeers and laughter, but in others, where natural powers of will and mind aid them, not ineffectual in hardening the thoughts of a hillside or the thoughts of a little group of men in the corner of a big town, making of them a rocky soil for newer ideas."

O'Leary died in what seemed, and not only to the poet Yeats, a base and sordid time that made brutal mockery of all ideals ever held or sacrifices made by noble revolutionaries. In his poem "September 1913" Yeats accused that time and asked the question that Irishmen in varying moods — anger, or mockery, or in that sour Irish humor that at one and the same moment can laugh at and sentimentalize about itself — will forever go on playing about with and seldom or never staying for an answer: *"Was it for this the wild geese spread/ The grey wing upon every tide;/For this that all that blood was shed,/For this Edward Fitzgerald died,/ And Robert Emmet and Wolfe Tone,/All that delirium of the brave?/Romantic Ireland's dead and gone,/It's with O'Leary in the grave."*

Yet in sober truth that tiger of a man, agitator, organizer, orator, James Larkin, defying William Martin Murphy and the Dublin employers who would, if they could, starve the Dublin workers into submission, was as fine a figure, and a deal more practical, than any great shadow out of the past, and behind Larkin there was the relentless purpose, the nobility, the capacity for self-sacrifice of James Connolly. In *The Irish Review* in 1913 Connolly, who three years later was also to die before the firing squad, wrote a passage that was at the core of all his

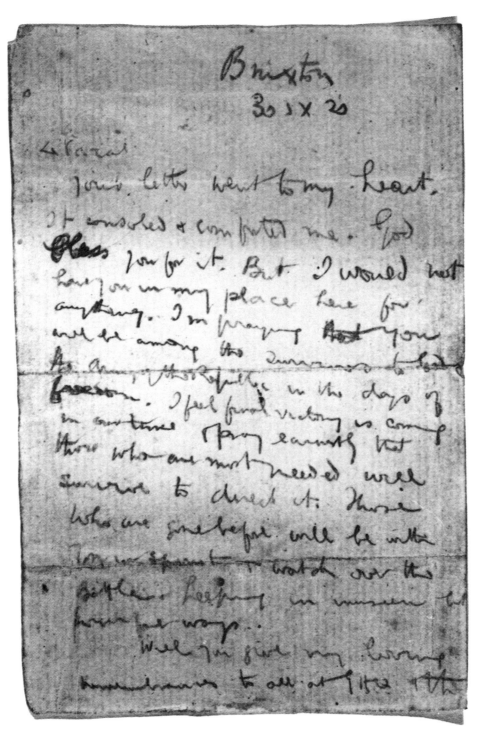

Brixton
30.IX.20

A Cathal
Your letter went to my heart. It consoled and comforted me. God bless you for it. But I would not have you in my place here for anything. I'm praying that you will be among the survivors to lead the Army of the Republic in the days of freedom. I feel final victory is coming in our time and pray earnestly that those who are most needed will survive to direct it. Those who are gone before will be with you in spirit to watch over the battle helping in unseen but powerful ways.

Will you give my loving remembrances to all at GHQ, and the officers and men of Dublin Brigade of whom we are all so proud and to the organization as a whole. Its work goes on splendidly.

Remember me specially to Mick C., Dick McKee, Diarmuid, Rory O'Connor, Gearoid, Austin—too many names come before me. But don't forget Leo Henderson. I'm sending a line to Dick M— too tired to go on.

Whatever I suffer here is more than repaid for by the fruit already reaped—if I die I know the fruit will exceed the cost a thousand fold. The thought makes me happy and I thank God for it.

Ah, Cathal, the pain of Easter Week is properly dead at last!

I wish I could say all that's in my heart to thank you for your beautiful letters. God guard and preserve you for the future. God bless you again and again and give you and yours long years of happiness under the victorious Republic. With all a comrade's love. God bless you.

Toirdhealbhac

Letter from Terence MacSwiney to Cathal Brugha, written after 46 days of hunger striking.

writings on Ireland's history and on Ireland's urgent need for a social and economic shake-up: "Ireland is a country of wonderful charity and singularly little justice. And Dublin being an epitome of Ireland it is not strange to find that Dublin, a city famous for its charitable institutions, should also be infamous for the perfectly hellish conditions under which its people are housed, and under which its men, women and children labour for a living . . . these things ought to be familiar to every true patriot; if they are not, it is a sure sign that their patriotism takes no stock of those things which make for or against the well-being and the greatness of a people."

That sort of talk was a long echo of the hunting horn away from heroes of ancient days in faery trance under historic hills or even from gallant gold-ringleted young men smiling their way to the gallows. But it was exactly in line with the labors of Michael Davitt, who had been the chief breaker of the feudal power of the landowners in Ireland, and with the sparse writings of that strange remote man, James Fintan Lalor, who had argued that God had granted the earth to Adam and his poor children forever and ever. Pearse had picked on Lalor, along with Tone, Mitchel and Davitt, as one of the evangelists of the gospel of Irish freedom.

Yet the poets were with the practical man, James

THE SACK OF CORK

Over Three Hundred Houses in Ruins

DEBRIS STREWN STREETS

Fire Brigade Grapple With Sporadic Outbreaks

Connolly, who had also a most poetic vision of Ireland in the coming times. George Russell (AE), who walked between the woods and hills of vision to organize farming cooperative societies, went to the Albert Hall in London to tell whoever cared to listen about the present state of Ireland and, in a famous open letter, told the Dublin employers about themselves and the sad state of their souls:

"You may succeed in your policy and ensure your own damnation by your victory. The men whose manhood you have broken will loathe you, and will always be brooding and scheming to strike a fresh blow. The children will be taught to curse you. The infant being moulded in the womb will have breathed into its starved body the vitality of hate. It is not they — it is you who are blind Samsons pulling down the pillars of the social order." He had used that same tone and style in an earlier letter to a fellow poet when Kipling, in verse by no means at his best, had made an ill-informed statement on the poisonous situation that the English Tories, by playing on old sectarian rancors, had created in the northeast of Ireland. He had written to Kipling: "You had the ear of the world and you poisoned it with bigotry and prejudice. You had the power of song and you have always used it on behalf of the strong against the weak." *(Continued on page 138)*

On the night of December 11, 1920, the city of Cork burst into
flames. First to burn was the principal street of shops, then the
City Hall and Free Library, and finally the fire was beyond
control. The British claimed that Cork citizens
had set the fire themselves.

Inscription written in the blood of victim bayoneted by the British.

King Street Barracks, Cork, after gutting by explosives.

Citizens of Cork picking through the rubble.

Scene of major destruction in Cork.

*Up to December, the British military had still officially been
engaged in a "police action." French had bridled, insisted his
power to maintain order was too restricted to be effective.
On December 10 he had proclaimed martial law in four major
counties, and one more county was soon to follow.*

So there was the threat of "violence upon the roads," that show of arms and of treason in the Orange northeast that was in turn to provoke the show of arms in Dublin and elsewhere. There was actual violence on the streets of Dublin and people bludgeoned by police acting as bullies for employers whose poison gas was hunger. Nor can William Martin Murphy be denied his fair place among the makers of the oratorical literature of the time. Charles Dickens, alas, lived too early to be influenced by Murphy's address to "my friends, the workers" when the workers were irresponsible enough to join a trades union and ask for a living wage; but Murphy could have polished his style by a careful study of Gradgrind in *Hard Times*. He said: "My friends — and I may truly call you my friends, because every employee of every undertaking that I am connected with I look upon as a friend . . . a strike in the tramway would, no doubt, produce turmoil created by the roughs and looters, but what chance would the men without funds have in contest with the Company which could and would spend £ 100,000 or more. You must recollect when dealing with a company of this kind that every one of the shareholders, to the number of five, six, or seven thousands, will have three meals a day whether the men succeed or not. I don't know," he added, "if the men who go out [on strike] can count on this."

He knew well that they could not. He promised his friends, the workers, starvation, or the raise of a shilling a week which was much the same thing, and half a day's pay to every man who came to hear him speak in the Antient Concert Rooms where not so long before Yeats's *The Countess Cathleen* had had its first performance and called forth the condemnation of a cardinal who hadn't read a blessed or unblessed line of it. Seven hundred men heard Murphy, and heard him say also that if they all said "God Save Ireland" and departed they would be doing a good day's work. A light day's work, he probably felt, for half a day's pay; yet the prayer that was in their seven hundred hearts was more than likely that God should save Ireland from Martin Murphy, and their deepest feelings would have been expressed in the words of a working man called Sean O'Casey, who in his time was to throw the agony and poetry and sour humor of those years onto the stage of the Abbey Theater and onto stages all over the world. O'Casey wrote: "Have a care, Marshal Murphy, starvation is not a pleasant anticipation, it is always a difficult thing to starve thousands unwilling to suffer where food is plentiful. Hunger makes men weak; it often makes men desperate, *(Continued on page 144)*

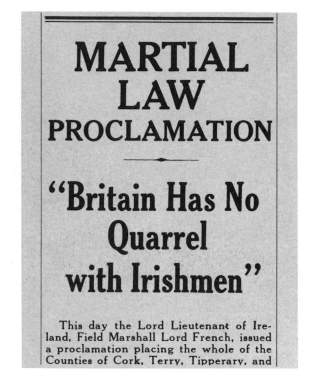

MARTIAL LAW PROCLAMATION

"Britain Has No Quarrel with Irishmen"

This day the Lord Lieutenant of Ireland, Field Marshall Lord French, issued a proclamation placing the whole of the Counties of Cork, Terry, Tipperary, and

(Right) Dublin Castle barricaded behind barbed wire for protection against night raids by the IRA

Scenes in Dublin under martial law: British troops enter city . . .

. . . Without notice, they round up citizens in the streets and conduct spot inspections for arms.

British Auxiliaries search a Post Office van.

Lacking sufficient troops to manage the disorder, the British
carried out reprisals against Republicans more or less at random.
Less haphazard, however, was their sabotage of Irish industry.
Over the summer of 1920 creameries, mills, and factories
were systematically burned down.

and the ferocity of hungry men and women is a dreadful thing."

Those were, indeed, hard times for those times, and the barometer was set for bloodshed. For all that was to follow it needed only a small number of determined men prepared to risk or throw away their lives: "To break their strength and die, they and a few, in bloody protest for a glorious thing." Pearse in his cell, waiting for death, put those words in a poem into the mouth of a mother, who, like his own mother, had lost two sons in a bloody protest of this kind: *"They shall be spoken of among their people,/The generations shall remember them/And call them blessed."*

There was a day in Dublin in 1916 when James Stephens the poet stood near the Shelbourne Hotel and looked through railings and over a hastily-built barricade into the park called, but not after the poet, St. Stephen's Green. "There were only the trees to be seen," he wrote, "and through them small green vistas of sward." He was a poet who had written of three centaurs playing upon a hill, stamping the ground in their power and pride and lust, of a wicked satyr creeping through a wood, of meditative goats following crooked paths through the furze. He might have seen the ancient gods. What he recorded in his eye-witness account, *The Insurrection in Dublin,* was that he saw a man walking across the street directly toward the barricade and attempting to pull out from that awkward structure a piece of his property. Then suddenly the park was alive not with centaurs or satyrs, but with young men carrying guns, threatening and warning that lonely indignant claimer of confiscated property, shooting him down on the street when threats and warnings had failed to make the poor man realize that he was really opposing himself to a revolution. James Stephens and some other people ran to the man's assistance, "while a woman screamed unmeaningly, all in one strident note. The man was picked up and carried to a hospital beside the Arts Club. There was a hole in the top of his head and one does not know how ugly blood can look until it has been seen clotted in hair." The ugliness of clotted blood, the horror of an unmeaning scream might stand symbolically for one aspect of the violent thing that burst upon the streets of the city in which James Stephens and some others had fed gloriously on verse and legend and high heroic story. But the violent thing was never utterly divorced from the suggestion of another world of poetry and color. Somewhere else during that week of fighting Stephens saw a boy with a revolver doing his routine revolutionary duty from a determination implanted previously on his imagination, but in a

(Above) Auxiliaries working to perfect their marksmanship.

(Right) Citizens being rounded up under British fire.

British secret service had expanded its activities so
far as to become, in the words of one British officer, merely
"a camouflaged institution having as its avowed object the
extermination of Sinn Fein 'Extremists.' " Most dangerous of its
agents lived as ordinary citizens in private houses in Dublin.

Detectives of the G Division, Dublin Metropolitan Police, confer outside the Dublin morgue after an inquest. Two of them
were soon to be shot dead in the streets.

way that showed plainly how completely his mind was then separated from the mechanical actions of his body: "Continually his eyes went searching widely, looking for spaces, scanning hastily the clouds, the vistas of the streets, looking for something that did not hinder him, looking away for a moment from the immediacies and rigours which were impressed where his mind had been."

The young volunteer soldier who was rapt in that way between the world of the gods and the realities of the world of revolution could have been thinking of Wolfe Tone or Owen Roe, or calling Cuchulain to his side, or rhyming over to himself any fragment of romantic verse or balladry, songs of the men of the west or of Henry Joy McCracken or John Kelly of Killane in 1798 or of the bold Fenian men in 1867. *"We've men from the North from the Nore and the Shannon,/Let the tyrant come forth we'll have force against force./Our tongue is the sword and our voice is the cannon,/Rifle 'gainst rifle and horse against horse."*

Or he could have been remembering a poem by that man of the people, William Rooney, or considering himself as the merry ploughboy of that song, forever popular with young Irishmen, who was marching with his comrades: *"Off to Dublin in the green and the blue,/Our helmets glitter in the sun./Our bayonets flash like lightning/To the rattle of the Thompson gun./It's the dear old flag of Ireland, boys,/That proudly waves on high,/And the password of our order is:/We'll conquer, or we'll die."*

Or on a more elevated literary level, the young man could have been thinking of lines of Lionel Johnson, who from his barstool in The Cheshire Cheese in London and the company of the "lost generation" of poets of whom he was one of the most notably lost, could write about Ireland as nobly as he had written about the statue of King Charles at Charing Cross: *"A terrible and splendid trust/Heartens the host of Innisfail:/Their dream is of the swift sword-thrust,/A lightning glory of the Gael./ "Croagh Patrick is the place of prayers,/And Tara the assembling place:/But each sweet wind of Ireland bears/The trump of battle on its race./ "From Dursey Isle to Donegal,/From Howth to Achill, the glad noise/ Rings: and the heirs of glory fall,/Or victory crowns their fighting joys./ "A dream! a dream! an ancient dream!/Yet, ere peace come to Innisfail,/Some weapons on some field must gleam,/Some burning glory fire the Gael."/*

Or was the boy that Stephens saw one of the young men sent out by (Continued on page 158)

*Collins felt British intelligence agents to be the greatest danger to
the Irish cause, and on Sunday morning, November 21, Collins's
Counter-Intelligence agents entered the house of fourteen
British agents and shot them dead . . .*

Collins's security squad.

*. . . Reprisals for the killings came that afternoon, when R.I.C. and
Black and Tans opened fire into a crowd of civilians watching a
football match in Croke Park, killing a dozen people and
wounding many more.*

Dublin Castle Intelligence Officers known to the IRA as "the murder gang." The men numbered 1, 2 and 3 were Irish.

TRAGIC WEEK-END IN DUBLI[N]

ELEVEN OFFICERS OF CROWN KILLED.

SIMULTANEOUS RAID IN MANY STREETS.

A BIG SENSATION.

RUNNING BATTLE IN LR. MOUNT ST.

FIERCE FIGHT ENSUES.

ONE WOUNDED CIVILIAN CAPTURED.

Yesterday the most tragic of the events which have recently happened in Ireland took place in Dublin, and resulted in the deaths of 27 persons, while a great many were wounded.

great tragedy commenced about 9 a.m., when civilian raiders entered a great many houses in various parts of the city, but particularly in the Lr. Mount St., Baggot St., Earlsfort Tce. districts, in which army officers and ex-officers resided, and, inquiring for them by names, demanded to be conveyed to their rooms, and 14 were shot dead and 5 wounded.

ttle in Mount Street.

Lower Mount St. the raiders were surprised by a body of Crown forces, and a regular battle ensued. The raiders endeavoured to escape by the back, but were fired on, and as one of them mounted a wall he was shot and rolled back, apparently badly wounded,

lians—came into the hallway. They produced revolvers and rushed to the first floor. After that I heard shooting."

Further inquiries elicited the following story:—When the men came into the hall 3 of them stood at the bottom of the stairway and the others went on to the first floor, where there are 3 bedrooms.

The room on the back was occupied by Mr. M'Mahon and another man and the door was not locked. One of the intruders, evidently the leader, opened the door and walked in. Mr. M'Mahon and his companion were in a large double bed in the centre of the room between two windows looking out on the back.

MR. M'MAHON'S FATE.

The leader, revolver in hand, walked over to the bed and, addressing Mr. M'Mahon, said: "Hello Mac, where are your guns?" Mr. M'Mahon, who was covered with the revolver, replied that they were in the drawer, and pointed to a chest of drawers at the wall.

The man walked over, pulled out the drawer, and took out two loaded revolvers. He then turned and walked towards the door where two other men were standing.

When near the door he turned again and, levelling his revolver, fired 3 or 4 shots at Mr. M'Mahon.

All the shots took effect, and Mr. M'Mahon partly lifted himself out of the bed and fell on the floor, where he lay.

Death must have been instantaneous, for he did not move. All the time his companion lay in the bed, terror-stricken and unable to move.

DOOR LOCK BLOWN AWAY.

While this was going on, another party of the intruders were attempting to enter the front room. The door was evidently locked, and resisted the attempts to open it.

When the shots had been fired in the back room, the men trying to force the door stood back a few paces on the landing and fired a volley of shots at the lock of the door, which was practically blown away.

Another attempt was made to force the door, but some heavy object was against it, and it resisted.

While this was going on a fusillade of shots broke out in the hallway, where 3 men were left standing.

apparently, other men, both sides taking the best possible cover, and at the same time continuing the battle.

BATTLE BREAKS OUT AFRESH.

One of the escaping civilians was about getting over the yard wall, when he was shot down. He lay in the yard under a small tree for nearly 1½ hours, until he was removed by the military, apparently in a dying condition. All the other retreating men escaped.

He could hear firing also in the house, and coming to a window overlooking the street he saw 4 young men, revolvers in hands, dash from the door of No. 22. They were fired on, and the fire was returned. Four or five more young men then dashed out, and hard on their heels came other men firing.

BULLETS WHIZZED: MEN STAGGERED

The escaping men zig-zagged on the street, fired, and a battle on a big scale developed for a few minutes.

Bullets whizzed about, and men on either side staggered as if hit, but clung on and continued the fight with the utmost grimness. Anything to equal it, said our informant, could hardly be conceived.

Smoke belched from the weapons, men on either side reloaded every now and then. The plan of the escaping men appeared to be to fight a retreat into Grattan St. Their pursuers were displaying all the tactics and manoeuvres of trained men with a view to closing in, but

the veritable hail of lead made death certain for anyone at close range. At no time was the range of fire less than 60 yards.

CONTACT LOST: FIRING CEASES.

Eventually the retreating men got into Grattan St. and away. One of the fugitives appeared to be wounded in the hand and dropped his revolver on the road. It was picked up by an opponent

They went into Grattan St. in pursuit, but contact was lost and the firing ceased.

An ex-army officer who also witnessed the battle on the street said he had seen some hot passages in France, but while it lasted in Mount St. such a strikingly daring and audacious stand-up fight he never saw.

He could see that one side in the use of their weapons displayed technique and training, whilst on the other this finish was not so apparent, but there was reckless daring, and coolness.

Crowds of persons using the thoroughfare fled in terror, and persons who were seen looking through windows were ordered

CROK

RAID ON MA

TWELV

WILD ST. CROWD

Terrifying sce[ne] yesterday a during the lenge footb teams repre Tipperary, auxiliary p pearance.

Volleys of rifle 15,000 specta ate attemp casualties t

SERIOUSL 54 OTHERS

An official acco forces went cerned in th morning, an raised an al approaching returned.

There were most quently when one of the wounded were to hospital.

AWFUL D

NAMES OF

Of 12 spectators to bullet wou died of bayonet was trampled other cases wer

-27 DEATHS.

FATHER GRIFFIN'S BODY FOUND IN A BOG.

PARK SHOOTINGS.

OTBALL

LLED.

EDE OF FIRE.

Rd. when the shooting had ceased and comparative quiet had been restored were confronted with big pickets of military, who had apparently taken over charge.

Everyone was subjected to a minute search, being first ordered to put up hands. People were compelled to keep their hands above their heads until they had reached the end of the road. Most of the men bore marks of the terrible experience.

Some were bleeding profusely from the face and hands; others were hatless, while more had their clothes torn and blood-spattered.

When the armed forces and armoured cars entered the field the scenes became indescribable, said another spectator. When the park was encircled the women and children were told they might go. The men were then all searched, and when any motion took place in the crowd a volley of shots were fired over their heads.

One of the collectors at the gate alleged that a bundle of notes, part of the receipts, were taken when he was being searched.

e witnessed
Park when,
s of a chal-
ch between
Dublin and
R.I.C., and
de their ap-

e heard, and
l in a desper-
scape. The
KILLED, 11
NDED, AND
ED.

s the Crown
persons con-
gs yesterday
that pickets
fired on the
he fire being

scenes subse-
who include
players, and
and removed

SEVENTEEN LORRIES.

A gentleman who was convenient to the grounds related how

about 17 lorries filled with Crown forces came dashing along, stopping about 20 yards from the canal bridge.

Dismounting, they opened fire. This gentleman saw a young lad with a wound on the left temple. Two men took the boy away. He next saw another man being taken up the street apparently dead. He was brought away on a car.

Some time later, St. Joseph's road was swept with bullets, and a man was shot. His body, said our informant, was put over the railings into an open space in front of the houses, and was still there at 6 p.m.

SICKENING SENSATION.

H-ROLL

VICTIMS.

9 succumbed
boy of 14
and a woman
Sixty-five
in city hos-
were injured

CROWDS RUSH FOR COVER

The effect of the first volley was sickening. Everybody rushed the entrance gates. The players, who, with those on the touch-line seats, seemed in the most exposed position, dashed off and mingled with the rushing crowd.

Panic-stricken though many were, the knot of people at the turn-stile leading to the side line seats were reassured by cries of " It is blank shot they're firing," accompanied by advice to keep low. They kept

ABDUCTED PRIEST'S TRAGIC FATE.

HIS BODY FOUND IN A BOG.

2 BULLET WOUNDS

MOST. REV. DR. O'DEA ON TRAGEDY.

GALWAY PEOPLE'S GRIEF

7 COTTAGES GUTTED AT BARNA.

The dead body of Rev. M. Griffin, B.A., C.C., who was abducted from his home in Galway on Sunday night, 14th inst., by 3 men wearing trench coats, was found buried in a bog at Clough-skella, about 4 miles from Galway, on Saturday night.

There was a bullet wound in the right temple, with another wound, apparently an exit one, higher up in the right temple. One eye was open, and the expression on the face is described as one of agonised determination.

How the Discovery Was Made.

The discovery, it is said, was made through parishioners following up inquiries regarding a motor vehicle which, it is stated, came towards Lough Inch from Shantalla on Monday at 11 p.m. and stopped near where the body was found.

rade," added Fr. O'Meehan. The men drew away, and there was a suppressed moan, followed by a growl of indignation and horror. ' In God's name be calm, boys,' I begged. ' Fr. Griffin is far better off than anyone, for he is in heaven.' I knew him to be a saint.' "

The body, continued Fr. O'Meehan, lay with the feet towards Galway, covered with about 2 feet of soil. It was clad just as he had left the house, but they could not find his hat. They rubbed away the gravel and mud from his face. The body was guarded throughout the night by a number of his parishioners, and was taken to Sea Rd., Galway, at 7 a.m. yesterday.

Questioned as to the expression on Fr. Griffin's face, Fr. O'Meehan said: " One of the eyes was open. There was an agonised expression on the face and an expression on the mouth as if he was framing a protest."

MYSTERIOUS MOTOR.

No evidence, he added, could be discovered near the scene to show that any shots had been fired there, and the presumption was that the dead body had been taken there in a motor. "It has been alleged," he continued, " that some young men in the district heard a lorry come along the road from Shantalla about 11 p.m. on Monday. The lights were extinguished near the cross roads, and after about 20 minutes the motor moved away, turning down towards Barna village."

A COLLEAGUE'S TRIBUTE.

" I would like to add," said Father O'Meehan, speaking with emotion, " that he has been my colleague and comrade for nearly two years, and I can say from my heart that I had never met or associated with, at home or in foreign lands, a nobler character, a truer soggarth, or a kindlier friend. His death in such circumstances will have a greater effect upon the conscience of the civilised world than even the martyrdom of the late Lord Mayor of Cork. May God have mercy on the murderers of the most innocent and child-like man I have ever known."

A STRANGE FACT.

It is a strange fact that whilst Father O'Meehan has received no fewer than threatening notices no message of the kind

Dublin Customs House, important center of British administration, was taken by the IRA on May 25, 1921, and completely gutted by fire. The IRA suffered a number of casualties and 80 were arrested.

Rounding up prisoners of Customs House battle.

Outside the Customs House: British await wagon to carry off body of dead IRA member.

*Lloyd George called for negotiations to reach some settlement
with the Irish. De Valera demanded a cessation of hostilities first,
and a truce between British and Irish armies was declared on
July 11, 1921. I.R.A. men returned to their homes pending
further orders.*

the play that Yeats afterwards worried about when he asked himself had that play of his sent out certain men the English shot? Katherine Tynan in an autobiographical volume, *The Years of the Shadow,* that seemed to be mostly in praise of the undeniable virtues of Lord and Lady Aberdeen, remembered a night when the play about that old woman who became young and walked like a queen, because young men were to die for her sake, was performed. It was an evening in March 1916, and the two plays on the Abbey Theater's oddly mixed bill were Yeats's *Cathleen ni Houlihan* and *The Mixed Marriage* of St. John Ervine. At the theater with Katherine Tynan and her husband were a young British Hussar officer and one of the Tynan boys on leave from the British military camp at Ballykinlar: "There was a fair amount of khaki through the house; and although people took it for granted that there would be a strong element of Sinn Fein amongst the Abbey audience, I don't think anyone had cause to feel uncomfortable because of the coat he wore. But the politics of the mass of the audience were pretty evident. The curtain went up for *Cathleen-ni-Houlihan.* There came the Little Old Woman creeping up to the cottage door, calling the bridegroom from the bride, the one that heard from the hearthfires and all that men love and desire, from

softness and pleasure and success and ease, to the hard path her lovers must tread. You could have heard a pin drop in the house. Then came: '*They shall be remembered for ever;/They shall be living for ever;/They shall be speaking for ever;/The people will hear them for ever./They have no need for prayers: they have no need for prayers.*' The gallery and the back of the house broke into tumultuous cheers and clapping of hands and the soldiers in khaki looked on wondering."

When the sixteen men were shot and the center of the city in ruins, William Yeats wrote in the poem "Easter 1916," that sums up a whole period and, once again, asks questions that have never been answered: *"This man had kept a school/And rode our wingèd horse;/This other his helper and friend/Was coming into his force;/He might have won fame in the end,/So sensitive his nature seemed/So daring and sweet his thought."*
But that teacher of a school and rider of the Irish Pegasus, and his fellow poet, and the other young poets among the men shot in Dublin had been possessed with a spirit, or a frenzy, away beyond poetry. A modern Irish poet, Robert Farren, speaks for them: *"No song had we but the heart's overflow,/The sad sweet cry of Eire to her sons,/Which answering we carried down the wind/To lure men's hearts to her."*

British Auxiliary mingles with Dublin crowd.

Arthur Griffith (left) and de Valera in London, where de Valera had gone to confer with Lloyd George.

With misgivings, but fearing a resumption of war, on December 6
Irish delegates signed treaty giving Ireland, to be called Irish Free
State, dominion status, and partitioning Ulster. Troubles lay
ahead, but British rule had been effectively brought to an end.

That old woman who had appeared in a bitter song of 1798, about the French being on the sea, had beckoned to the poets who had seen her as a young queen. She promised them nothing but the austere joy of that bloody protest for a glorious thing, and a failure in death that would mean the resurrection of a people. Their mood was one aspect of the dreaming that Shaw had his Larry Doyle inveighing against in *John Bull's Other Island.* It also went back to the poetry that was the broken cry of the Gaelic people and that could have the poet, the Hon. Emily Lawless, at the end of the 19th century, writing of that mother who had given her sons nothing but who was yet followed by their relentless love. Such dreams and passions, the revolutionary ideas and memories of a century, the urgent political and economic needs of the present, all made what was to happen seem so inevitable that the power of all opposition was considered as nothing measured against the protest of even one man, or the words and the death of one poet.

In one of his short plays, *The Singer,* Pearse had a mystical young wanderer, MacDara, cry out: "And so it is a foolish thing. Do you want us to be wise? . . . One man can save a people as one man redeemed the world." In a poem, "The Fool," he had the fool speak out, because the wise men had not, and say: "This I have heard in my heart, that a man shall scatter not hoard." It is in the mood of the last great lines of Yeats's *The Green Helmet,* where the hero offers to the man from the sea his head and his life in order to redeem his word and to save the honor of his people, and the man from the sea, instead of beheading him, crowns him as chief hero and chooses "the laughing lip that shall not turn from laughing," and, "the hand that loves to scatter, the life like a gambler's throw." General Maxwell had not the same sporting instincts and would have been less likely to approve of Yeats than of George Moore when Moore asked, what was General Maxwell to do: give the rebels prizes for good conduct? It was unlikely that the General could have grasped that when he had the poets and others shot he was, so to speak, playing into their hands by coming out of the sea to fulfill their prophecies. Pearse had, he wrote, set his face to the road before him: *"To the deed that I see,/to the death I shall die."* Joseph Mary Plunkett had seen a symbolic crucifixion in the red of the rose, in the stars, in the rain and snows, in the flowers and birdsong; and every thorn was part of the crown of thorns, every tree a cross. Thomas MacDonagh had written of a poet patriot that: *"His deed was a single word,/called out alone/In a night when no echo stirred/To laughter or moan./ "But his songs new souls shall thrill,/The loud harps dumb,/And his deed the echoes fill/When the dawn is come."*

Casement, *"hanged to the tolling of a bell,"* as Padraic Colum wrote, *"and their Smiths and their Murrays and their Cecils say it's well,"* had known and said that he could have followed another path that would have led to comfort and honors. It was indeed, as MacDara had cried out, a foolish thing but it had the desired and prophesied effect, and Yeats when he had asked the still unanswered question went on to acknowledge forever that truth: *"Was it needless death after all?/For England may keep faith/For all that is done and said./We know their dreams; enough/To know they dreamed and are dead;/And what if excess of love/Bewildered them till they died?/I write it out in a verse—/MacDonagh and MacBride/And Connolly and Pearse/Now and in time to be,/Wherever green is worn,/Are changed, changed utterly:/A terrible beauty is born."* □

(Right) Signatures affixed to the treaty instrument.

18.   This instrument shall be submitted forthwith by His
Majesty's Government forthe approval of Parliament and by
the Irish signatories to a meeting summoned for the
purpose of the members elected to sit in the House of
Commons of Southern Ireland, and if approved shall be
ratified by the necessary legislation.

~ 6ᵗᵉ 1921

On behalf of the
British Delegation.

D Lloyd George

Austen Chamberlain

Birkenhead.

Winston S. Churchill,

L. Worthington Evans

On behalf of the Irish
Delegation

Ａrt Ó Gríobhtha (Arthur Griffith)

Mícheál Ó Coileáin

Riobárd Barton

E. S. Duggan

Seoirse Gabhán uí Dhubhthaigh

Contributors

Eamon de Valera, President of Ireland, has helped to guide the destiny of his country and its citizens from Easter Week 1916 to the present.

Thomas P. O'Neill is a noted Irish historian who has recently completed a biography of President de Valera.

Padraic Pearse, poet, playwright and teacher, was a major figure in modern Irish nationalism and a leader of the Easter Uprising. He was executed by the British on May 3, 1916.

James Connolly, leader of the Irish Transport and General Workers' Union and Commandant of the Irish Citizen Army, was Commander of the Republican forces in Easter week. He, too, fell before a British firing squad—on May 12, 1916.

Sean T. O'Kelly, a leading figure in the Irish Volunteers and Sinn Fein, served as President of Ireland from 1945 to 1959.

Benedict Kiely, novelist and critic, has written frequently on Irish literature in publications throughout the English-speaking world.

Goddard Lieberson is president of Columbia Records and Producer of the CBS Legacy Collection.

Photo Credits

The CBS Legacy Collection

Bernard Farbar, Director
Midge Podhoretz, Editor
Ira Teichberg, Art Director